# Designing Creative Resumes

Gregg Berryman

Revised Edition

Crisp Publications
1200 Hamilton Ct.
Menlo Park, CA 94025

Crisp Publications, Inc.
1200 Hamilton Court
Menlo Park, CA 94025-1427

ISBN 1-56052-605-X
04 10 9 8 7 6 5 4 3

**Library of Congress Cataloging-in-Publication Data**
Berryman, Gregg, 1942-
Designing creative resumes / Gregg Berryman.—Rev. ed.
p. cm.
Includes bibliographical references.
ISBN 1-56052-605-X (pbk.)
1. Resumes (Employment) I. Title.
HF5383 .B43 2002
650.14'2--dc21
2001007312

# Contents

# Acknowledgements

Dedicated to my wife Phyllis for her help and support throughout this project.

Many thanks to the creative professionals, most of them my former students, for their consent to reprint the resume samples shown in this book, to Gaylord Bennitt for the portrait illustration on the back cover, and to all the production personnel at Crisp Learning for their patience and encouragement.

Design: Gregg Berryman
Cover: Fifth Street Design
Manuscript: Phyllis Berryman
Editor: George Young
Typography: Nicole Phillips
Printer: Von Hoffmann Graphics, Inc.
Type: American Typewriter, Helvetica

# Introduction

Resumes are used by job seekers of all types to help them land or change employment. Millions of these important documents are produced annually but most have little verbal or visual impact. In fact most resumes are, to say the least, forgettable.

This book is about a special kind of resume, the creative resume. Employers of creative professionals are inevitably articulate and particular. These busy executives spend a part of every workday producing persuasive words and images. They are by nature critical and demanding. An average resume makes little impact on them. However, a creative resume can attract the attention of creative managers and provoke their prompt response.

Your creative resume should be exceptional. It must elevate you above the crowd and clearly show that you can produce results. It should link your needs with those of a potential employer. Above all, your creative resume must stimulate the employer to meet and interview you.

Like most creative professionals, you may assemble many resumes during your career. The first might be for an internship, cooperative work experience, or summer job. Later when you seek a full-time entry-level position, the resume becomes a critical part of your job search package. Whenever you change your employment an updated resume is necessary. The resume might also be used effectively when consulting or applying for grants and fellowships.

The creative resume is a special tool. It establishes your credibility. It leaves a lasting impression. The creative resume is a crisp self-advertisement, a polished mirror of you. It establishes your personal identity in the mind of the employer. The creative resume must show you as a direct benefit to the company, organization, or institution. Remember, the first thing it must do is help to get you an interview.

# Resume Contents

Resume contents will vary from one individual to another. Your data are unique. Emphasize this fact. Beware of the packaged resume produced by resume services. These have a tendency to be equalizers. The creative resume is built on individual differences rather than similarities. Strive to be concise yet distinct. Employers are interested in your unique talents.

You need to develop an exceptional resume to help stage your creative interview. It must stimulate an employer to meet and interview you. It should make an unforgettable visual impression. It must establish your credibility, document your past and predict your future. Your creative resume needs to identify you and your work after the interview when you and your portfolio are no longer present.

What direction should your resume take? Certainly package yourself as a unique creative individual. Clarify the benefits an employer will realize when hiring you. Select a comfortable format that will help deliver critical data.

The **reverse chronological** (latest data first) format places emphasis on your most recent education, employment, and activities. This is an excellent approach for young designers with limited experience, as it helps focus on the leading edge of your career development. The reverse chronological format features strategic titles briefly embellished with responsibilities and accomplishments.

An interesting version of this format is the **timeline** resume which accounts for a specific portion of your career (usually 10 years). The timeline, organized as a matrix, is effective for demonstrating consistent progress towards a goal over an extended period. This resume format offers a fertile option for aspiring exhibit, publication, or environmental graphic designers, as timeline interpretation is quite common in these specialized areas.

Use the **narrative** resume format to tell an interesting story about yourself. This style allows you to de-emphasize facts and dates while featuring process and results. Narrative resumes present an opportunity to demonstrate excellent writing. A word ad, script, or storyboard for yourself might establish a logical narrative direction. Explore this format if your objective is to work in advertising, publications, film, animation, or the electronic media.

The **achievement** (functional) resume format is generally more useful for experienced rather than young designers. You focus on positive accomplishments including leadership responsibilities, funds managed, or goals met. Job titles, work history, and repetitive positions are subordinate to verifiable results. Designers find this resume format more useful for redirecting their career or aspiring to a senior position. The **endorsement** resume fits into this category and includes direct, attributed (usually glowing) quotes about your work performance.

To maximize your leverage on a specific design position consider a **targeted** resume. This format requires your all-out effort because a separate unique resume is created for each position. Targeted resumes depend on solid research and desktop technology. By careful editing you can make a powerful case for a specific job, eliminating data that would be necessary on a more general document.

| | | |
|---|---|---|
| ***achieved*** | ***evaluated*** | ***planned*** |
| ***analyzed*** | ***gained*** | ***prepared*** |
| ***arranged*** | ***generated*** | ***presented*** |
| ***created*** | ***implemented*** | ***produced*** |
| ***conducted*** | ***improved*** | ***promoted*** |
| ***constructed*** | ***increased*** | ***realized*** |
| ***coordinated*** | ***interpreted*** | ***researched*** |
| ***delivered*** | ***managed*** | ***strengthened*** |
| ***designed*** | ***motivated*** | ***supervised*** |
| ***developed*** | ***narrated*** | ***tested*** |
| ***directed*** | ***negotiated*** | ***trained*** |
| ***established*** | ***operated*** | ***upgraded*** |
| ***exhibited*** | ***organized*** | ***utilized*** |

# Employment Objective

IDENTIFICATION

OBJECTIVE

EDUCATION

EXPERIENCE

INTERNSHIPS

AWARDS

PUBLICATIONS

HONORS

COMPUTER

MEMBERSHIPS

LANGUAGES

TRAVEL

REFERENCES

A short, to-the-point job objective is appropriate when you apply for a specific internship or position beyond entry level. If you decide to use a placement agency, the job objective is necessary to link you with potential employers. It helps target your employment more exactly. By listing Corporate Design Manager, Senior Package Designer, or Digital Illustrator as your job objective you gain priority consideration for matching job titles. Avoid multi-sentence or full paragraph job objectives. They tend to confuse the employer rather than clarify your intentions.

When seeking your first career position, treat the job objective carefully. Consider excluding it from the resume, including it instead in your cover letter where you can target a job and a specific individual.

By mentioning a job objective on your resume you may be taking yourself out of the running for some positions with real potential. The job search process often uncovers positions very different from your original target. The job objective that begins as functional information may turn into a burden on the creative resume.

# Personal Information

Present clearly on the resume your name, address, and telephone number. Include your e-mail, fax, and website if available. Don't forget the zip code portion of the address. Remember that most interview appointments and other negotiations are conducted by telephone. Area code is important. Personal information must be easy to locate with a quick visual scan.

A resume listing two telephone numbers or addresses can be confusing and annoying. Yet certain situations, like residential moves, vacations, or extended travel, may make backup information seem inviting. Ask yourself "Will a phone call to my primary address reach me the same day if I am not there to answer it?" If "Yes," then a single address and phone number is sufficient.

During vacations or extended travel keep potential employers notified of your location with telephone or e-mail messages. Your work availability date may become an important entry on the creative resume.

Additional personal information should be weighed carefully. Employers are prevented by law from requesting age and marital status, but if your research shows that an employer prefers younger or married employees, such data might fit in. Listing birthdate (9-15-80) is more efficient than indicating your age in years (25) because it doesn't render your resume obsolete at your next birthday. Marital status can also change quickly. Most job seekers consider themselves healthy, so this information may best be left out. Handicaps may be discussed in the interview. Omit your draft status except in time of conflict.

Personal interests may give you extra dimension, particularly if they relate to your target position. Two or three personal interests, sports, or hobbies suggest real involvement. Including more items may indicate a lack of focus. When in doubt, leave personal interests out of the creative resume.

# Education/ Training

Education is a vital resume topic when you search for an internship, co-op position, or your initial job. It often diminishes in importance as you gain significant work experience.

Your alma mater brands you with a certain identity. Alumni networks and associates of your professors will usually give you an edge in the job search. Your performance in college predicts your job performance. Educational references on the creative resume demand clarity, consistency, and strategic position.

List your educational data in reverse chronological order. This sequence insures that your latest experience is read first. Include your college degrees, with dates conferred. Group the significant courses in your major and minor emphases. Arrange the courses precisely in your order of preference. Consider which special courses felt particularly challenging and comfortable. Place these at the top of your list to suggest a work preference. Adjust the sometimes lengthy and obscure titles of academic courses to fit common professional terminology. Omit nonspecific foundation courses from the creative resume.

Some educators have a high regional, national, or international profile. Concentrated study with such an individual or faculty team may open special doors. Mention of select high-profile teachers can give your creative resume an edge.

Forget high school as a resume listing. Consider doing the same for community or junior college unless your AA Degree has unusual significance. Simple mention of the two-year institution and degree date is adequate.

When listing colleges and degree dates, include the years but omit months and days. Your creative resume will be easier to scan and digest. Anticipated graduation dates can be legitimately listed.

Extraordinary class standing or grade point average should be woven in. If only average, omit this data on the resume and save it for your interview. If you earned 50-100% of your college expenses, don't hesitate to mention this. Employers are favorably impressed by self-starting students who cover their personal education costs.

Scholarships and fellowships earned should be listed in this or a separate category. These awards place you in select company and help you stand out, as does your command of a foreign language. Travel study programs add breadth to your educational experiences and fit the creative resume.

3.89

# Seminars/ Workshops

Significant extension courses, workshops, and training programs add depth to your capabilities. Seminars increase your professional exposure outside the college framework. Listed on the creative resume, they chart your desire for self-improvement. Continuing education suggests a positive growth curve. It reflects your desire to remain current with the trends and technology of the Information Age.

Mention your working knowledge of software, script writing, account management, or business practice. These skills add to your value. Participation in photography, video, computer, and photomechanical training programs offered by industry should be noted.

Indicate that the workshops listed on your creative resume had substance. Merely attending a two-hour lecture doesn't count. A weeklong or weekend of intense hands-on involvement does. If the workshop altered your outlook, opened new creative doors, and provided you with knowledge you can demonstrate, be sure to include it. Listings should be recent. Be ready to discuss attributes of such experiences with target employers.

***AIA Conventions***
***AIGA Conferences***
***American Center for Design Conferences***
***ASID Conferences***
***Aspen Design Conferences***
***Art Directors' Club Events***
***Broadcast Designers Conferences***
***CASE Seminars***
***Catalyst Management Seminars***
***Design Management Institute Conferences***
***Friends of Calligraphy Workshops***
***GATF Seminars***
***Graphic Artists' Guild Seminars***
***HOW Design Conferences***
***IABC Conferences***
***ICOGRADA Conferences***
***IDSA Conferences***
***Illustrators' Workshops***
***Kodak Technical Seminars***
***MacWorld Expos***
***Nikon Workshops***
***RIT Technical Seminars***
***SEGD Conferences***
***Seybold Conferences***
***SIGGRAPH Conferences***
***Stanford Publishing Conferences***
***TED Conferences***
***UCDA Conferences***
***University Extension Courses***
***Women in Communication Conferences***

# Work Experience

Employment History, Work Experience, Professional Experience, Work History, Experience, and Employment are alternative headings with similar meanings. Employers carefully scrutinize your past jobs. Show the positions you have held in reverse chronological order, latest to earliest. Your present position will attract the most attention at the top of the list.

Show the date of position, job title, and employer. Include the city and state of your employer. Omit the employer street address and telephone number as trivial.

A long list of previous jobs should be edited to those of interest to the target employer. Be sure to account carefully for the four or five years preceding your job search. Remember to include military positions with a stress on promotions, leadership responsibility, and acquired skills.

Your resume for an internship or first professional position may demand lumping together summer or part-time jobs. If you ever held two or three jobs concurrently, use this fact to your advantage. Employers are impressed with the organization and energy required to juggle multiple positions. Use language and style to place short-term positions in a good light.

Volunteer and field-work experiences have a place on the creative resume as long as the work you did was clearly significant. Did your efforts affect the organization, improve a program, or increase funding? Stress that your volunteer activities required interaction with people. Show that your group achieved a well-defined goal. Cooperative efforts closely parallel the job requirements of a creative position. Employers seek team players.

Work on a political campaign might be significant in your view. Some employers will have opposite political leanings. Include partisan experiences with great caution as they may cause awkward controversy.

On the creative resume you can do more than simply list positions held. Amplify your job titles list with a tight description of special skills acquired. List your accomplishments. Use a clear, concise style. Begin sentences with action verbs that feature leadership and organizational skills. "Developed," "supervised," "designed," "created," and "managed" help to build compact sentences that portray you as a doer.

# Internships/ Co-Ops

Internships, apprenticeships, and co-op positions differ from normal jobs. Although sometimes paid, the essence of such employment is on-the-job training. Employers recognize that interns have had exposure to the daily experiences of a studio or office. At best, co-op positions give an organization a close-up look at a potential employee under fire. Little wonder that many graduates gain their first full time jobs after positive performance in these positions.

Internships should be listed on the resume in the same style as normal jobs. In reverse chronological order show date, job title, employer, city, and state. With action verbs, detail your responsibilities and acquired skills.

If you have held several internships, consider fitting them under a separate heading of the same name. An alternative is to integrate internships under the Work Experience heading. If you choose this approach, be sure that the position is clearly labeled as internship or co-op. Any deception here, even if accidental, will reduce the impact of your creative resume.

# Awards/ Memberships

The creative resume should include a category (or categories) to list fellowships, scholarships, memberships, exhibitions, awards, publications, and productions. Your early resumes might be skeletal in these areas, but later versions will probably flesh out. Headings for these items should be logical. "Fellowships" and "Scholarships" may be paired. "Exhibitions" and "Awards" fit together, as do "Publications" and "Productions."

The fellowships and scholarships you list should have been earned in competition. Naturally more prestige is attached to grants from national organizations or professional societies. List the year of the award, its title, and its source. Including the financial value of a grant is optional, but is logical for very large dollar amounts.

Memberships have a place on the creative resume. You can show an employer that you function well as part of a group. Most positions require a similar interaction and team orientation. Your active participation in a student design, marketing, or communication club indicates a genuine professional orientation. Many national professional societies have student chapters. Regional design organizations, art directors' clubs, and advertising or marketing societies encourage student membership. Get involved and record it on your creative resume.

Social and service fraternities may have a place on the creative resume if you played an important leadership or management role. Mere membership is hardly worth listing. Sometimes the Greek names of fraternal organizations can be confusing to an employer. Yet if the employer is a sorority or fraternity alum you may get special consideration. The creative resume that stresses social activities at the expense of professional involvement is misguided.

Exhibitions and awards must be kept in perspective on the resume. National competitions are important. Local student shows are usually not, unless they have been juried by professionals and you have won an award. A one-person show of your work can be significant. List the year of the show, its title, its location, and the award you received on your creative resume.

Publications seldom appear on the resume created for an internship or first position. On later resumes, evidence of your published writing or visual work may be expected or even required. Publication in a student magazine or local newspaper doesn't count for much. Significant publication in a professional magazine, annual, or journal should be listed. Indicate date, publication, title of piece, and perhaps a brief description if the title is obscure. Have a tear sheet or photocopy in your portfolio.

Productions may advance your cause if your creative resume is slanted toward computer graphics, multi-media, film, or video. Your graduate thesis production qualifies. Date, production, title, credits, and a brief description of the piece are appropriate. Be prepared to screen your listed creative productions at your interview.

# Personal References

While in college you are developing resume references among the professors you impress with your performance. References may also come from the supervisor on your part-time job or the professional you work with in your internship position. Three strong references are enough.

Be sure to ask permission to use a reference's name. Confirm the address, telephone and e-mail address that you list. Some positions require written reference letters, but most do not. Virtually all contact between employer and reference is by telephone, so include a home phone number as a backup. Employers may become frustrated if they cannot easily reach people you've listed as references. It is considered good protocol to promptly notify a reference when an employer is about to call. This "heads-up" can also lead to a more positive telephone recommendation on your behalf. Keep track of your references; know when they'll be traveling or on vacation.

Reference listings should be kept discrete on the creative resume. A simple statement like "References furnished upon request" is sufficient. Back up this listing with a separate sheet or card containing complete reference data. Match the type style and paper color to your resume. Keep these separate reference pieces handy for interviews or mailing.

Do not list the names, addresses, and telephone numbers of references on your resume. The same is also true for a website resume. Extraneous calls may invade the privacy of your references. You may want to make a change in references due to a move, sabbatical leave, position change, or even a death. Also, high-powered references can distract an employer from the focus of the resume—you. By cultivating them and tracking them well, you can make references a valuable tool in your job search. A strong reference base is essential to the creative resume.

Mention here should be made of "To whom it may concern:" reference letters. No matter how complimentary, these documents or excerpts from them are far too generic to include as part of your creative resume package. However in some employment situations, sealed reference letters addressed specifically to an art director, principal, or hiring committee may be required.

# Resume Design

A maximum design effort separates the creative resume from common fact sheets. Resume design is too often overlooked or undervalued by otherwise well-prepared job seekers. Treat it like any important design task. Work at the top of your ability. Push the leading edge of your creativity. Since the resume is often your last creative piece before you accept a new position, strive to make it your best effort.

Consider how your resume will be received, handled, and stored by a potential employer. When delivered by hand, it must establish a quick positive impression. An employer often scans your resume during the interview. Critical information must be clear and easy to locate.

If you intend to mail your resume to a potential employer, think of it as a package begging to be opened. Design it for folding if you want it to arrive in a business-size envelope. To avoid a crushed, bent, or dimpled look, ship it in a rigid envelope, box, or mailing tube. Make a strong visual impression with the mailed resume to insure that it reaches your specific target employer. Avoid giving your resume package the appearance of junk mail. You don't want it to be dropped in the round file without being read.

PRIORITY MAIL

Pay attention to mailing details. Address the envelope to a specific person in the target firm. Include their job title. Match the type style of your cover letter if that is to be included in the package. Remember to supply your current return address. Select postage stamps rather than use a postal meter. Consider well-designed commemoratives that reflect your visual sensitivity and complement the envelope color. Rubber stamp the package with "First Class Mail," "Priority Mail," or "Do Not Bend," as appropriate. Above all make the package appear to contain the important business that it does—your resume.

Resumes are most often stored in files with letters and other documents. In corporations and job-placement firms, active files contain hundreds or even thousands of resumes—often scanned. Design your creative resume to fit common storage systems; otherwise it may be excluded from consideration.

Virtually all resumes are designed to the 8-1/2 x 11 inch format. If you need more space for resume contents add additional pages by folding. Avoid sizes and shapes that extend outside the edges of file folders. Even if your odd-sized resume manages to get filed, it will probably wind up with tattered edges. Smaller resume sizes easily fit filing systems but are difficult to retrieve and may get buried inside. Strive to design your resume so well that it will be tacked to the bulletin board in the design studio.

Once you understand how your resume is likely to be received, handled, and stored, your design task begins. The resume's essence is your unique information. Write, rewrite, and edit your resume's contents; then establish hierarchy. Prioritize the information. Explore positions on the format page that the employer will find logical. Make sure that all important facts can be picked up in a brief scan. Most obvious should be your name, address, and telephone, e-mail and website. Arrange the Education, Experience, Personal, Awards, and Membership information blocks to fit your unique profile. Your ability to organize information on the creative resume will make a strong impression on employers.

Type size is an important design consideration. However you choose to typeset the resume, beware of selecting extremely small type. Most employers will find 8-, 9-, and 10-point body type comfortable to read, while 4-, 5-, or 6-point will prove painful.

Your creative resume should blend form and content in a unique manner. It should convey your design philosophy and career direction. If your goal is publication design, the resume might take on a vertical, editorial look, stressing columns and complementary heads. An advertising resume might resemble a full-page ad with stress on a creative headline and an integrated photo or illustration. A calligrapher might blend elegant hand-lettered headlines with appropriate body type. If you seek a corporate design position, perhaps treat the resume as an annual report page with chronology and graphs. A copy editor might develop a resume resembling a manuscript, complete with proofreader marks.

A strong concept should underpin your creative resume. It can help overcome rather ordinary data. Powerful, direct communication is necessary. Try out your ideas on friends in brainstorming sessions. Work closely with a teacher or creative professional to develop design directions. Ask for feedback while you refine your strongest concept. Handle your final resume idea with finesse. Remember that the distance between the appropriate and the absurd is often quite narrow.

Each creative resume will take a unique visual direction. The resume's visual appearance should mirror your distinct creativity. As the information content of the resume reflects your personal history, its visual content predicts your career.

# Ideation Sketches

Ideation sketches help you to think on paper. You transform ideas into visual reality with these structured doodles. Thumbnail techniques are easy to master and are useful for developing the creative resume. These idea sketches are small but in proportion to the printed piece. If your resume is 8-1/2 x 11 inches, your thumbnails might be one quarter, one-third, or one-half that size. Try some at each size to explore the visualizing format that feels most comfortable to you.

The reduced size of thumbnail sketches allows you to create many in a short time. Each sketch should take but a few minutes to complete. Think in color, using your pencils, pens, and markers. Produce lots of ideas. Don't crowd them on the sheet. Allow each sketch to "breathe" with ample surrounding space on the page. Empty your brain. Never reject an idea until you probe it thoroughly with sketches.

Small sketches have an advantage. They don't involve detail that might interfere with your resume idea. Type can be indicated quickly with simple lines. You can experiment with a variety of type formats, composition, systems, and layouts. To speed development of the most promising thumbnails, trace over them. Design and refine as you repeat the tracing process to develop your creative resume.

Most significant graphic design doesn't happen by hit or miss. Communication excellence usually results from the development of visual alternatives. Thumbnail techniques help you refine your ideas. Keep your resume sketch size and style consistent so you will be able to compare your sketches. Tack the sketches on the wall side-by-side. Your best ideas will certainly emerge. Invite critical feedback from others at this stage in the process.

How many thumbnails should you do? Certainly more than a few. Give yourself the chance to explore several ideas. Use the tracing process to develop your creative resume. A unique resume layout will probably not emerge immediately. Be patient! Devote a little time and effort to the task. Flow with the process. Soon an original mini-resume will appear. While moderate in scope, the creative resume is certainly one of the most important design problems you will ever solve.

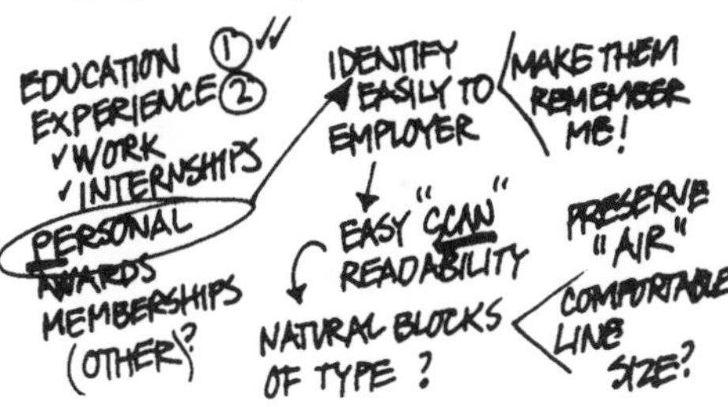


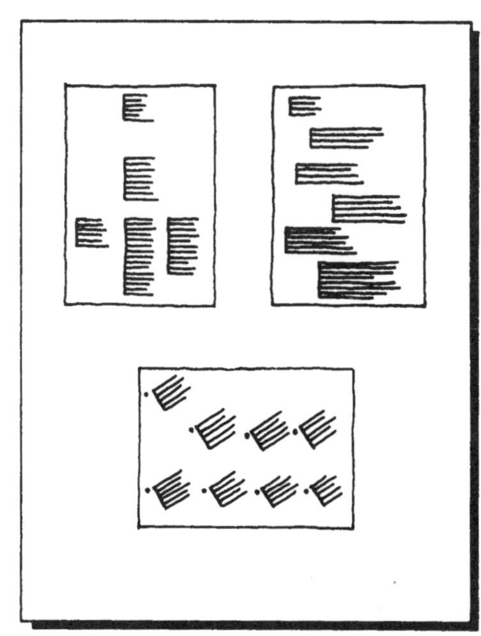

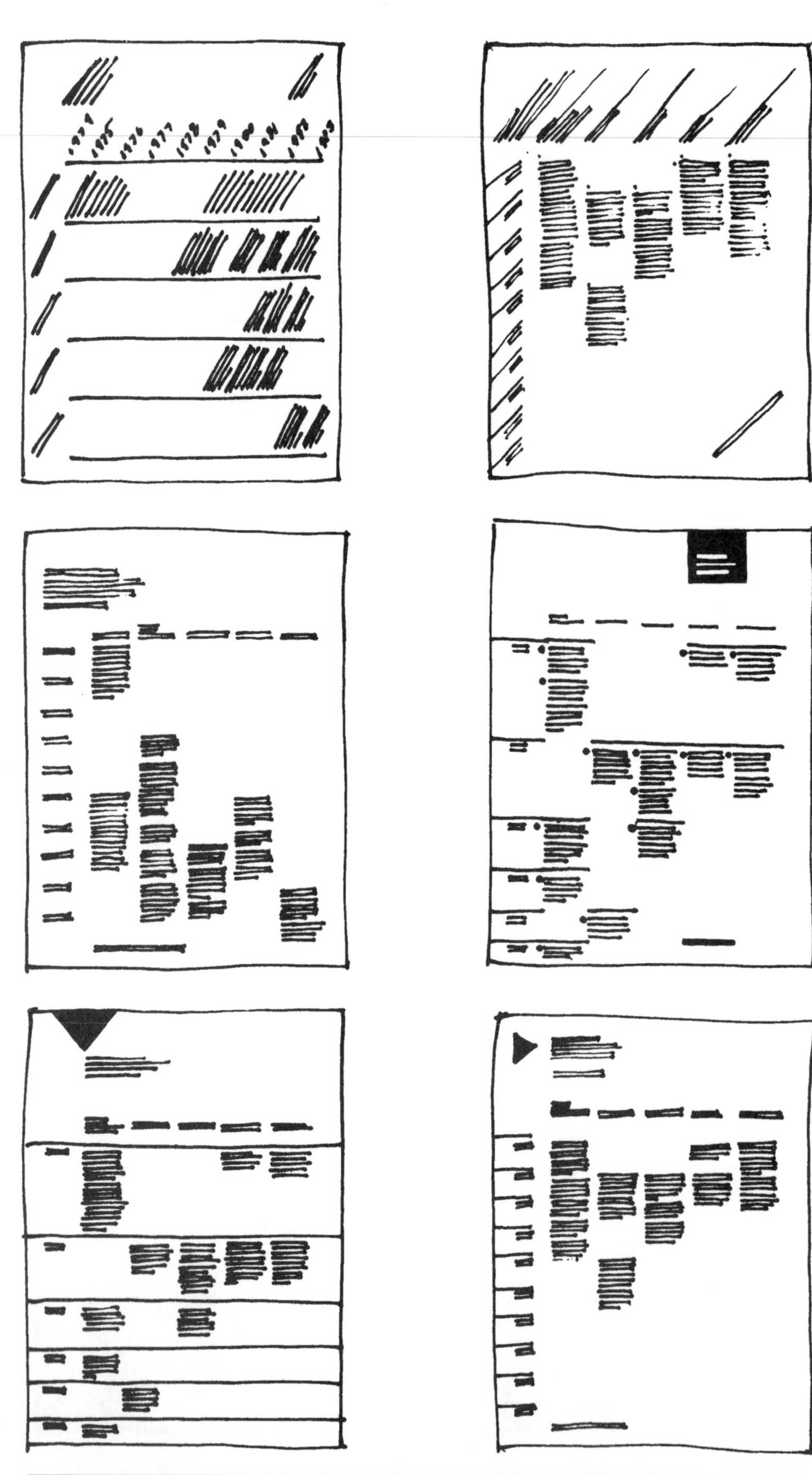

# Resume Mock-Ups

Consider direct mock-ups as an alternative to thumbnail sketches during the design process. The mock-up technique shortcuts design time. It is recommended for those who lack refined sketching skills. The mock-up process demands that all design decisions be made at real size. It reduces your margin for error.

The role of type in the design demands priority focus as you mock-up alternatives. Work with a simulated copyblock (sometimes called greeking) at 8-, 9-, or 10-point. Be sure the copyblock word count approximates that of your resume. Position the information blocks with a digital layout program to test your ideas. Copy can be repositioned quite easily. This mock-up technique will show you a fairly precise layout before final typesetting.

Another useful technique is to typeset your resume data first to a functional line length of 30 to 50 characters. Paste up the laserprinted type on blank sheets to simulate your printed resume. Many readable resume mock-ups can be assembled in a short time and at a low cost.

By designing with the type elements at real size you get a close replica of your final resume. Use the full capabilities of this inexpensive process to help you make decisions for the final resume.

Photocopies and color printouts on a variety of papers help to test your layout variations at low cost. Use the full capabilities of desktop printers to help you arrive at your creative resume.

●Temporibud autem quinsud et aur office debit
err epudiand sint et molestia non recusand.
delectus au aut prefer endis dolorib asperiore
quid est cur verear ne ad eam non possing accommodare
memorite tum etia ergat. Nos amice et nebevol,

●Endium neque nonor imper ned libiding gen
nulla praid om undant. Improb pary minuit, potius
dodecendesse videanteur. Inviat igitur vera ratio
Neque hominy infant aut inuiste

●Tia benevolent sib conciliant et, aptiss
omning null sit caus peccand quaert en irnigent
explent sine julla inura autend inanc sunt is parend non
Concupis plusque in ipsinuria detriment est quam in
Itaque ne iustitial dem rect quis dixer per se
am dilig et carum esse iucund est propter and

●Hancetiam mag quod cuis. Guae ad erat amicos
expetend quam nostras expetere quo loco videtur
tuent tamet eum locum seque facil, ut mihi detur
dictum est, sic amicitiand neg posse a luptate discedere.

●Etfirmatur animuset a spe pariender luptam seiung
despication adversantur luptabit, sic amicitiao

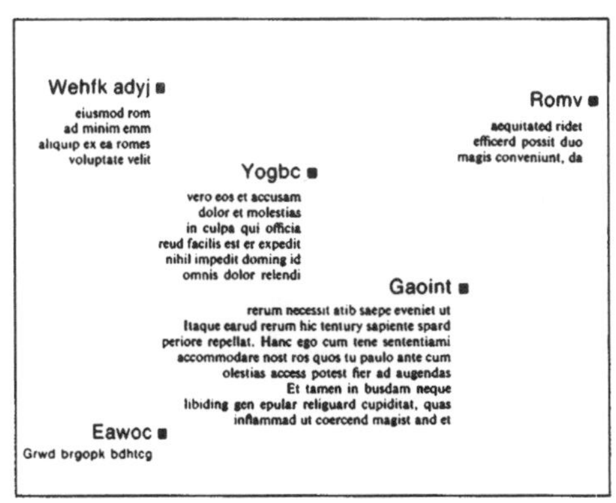


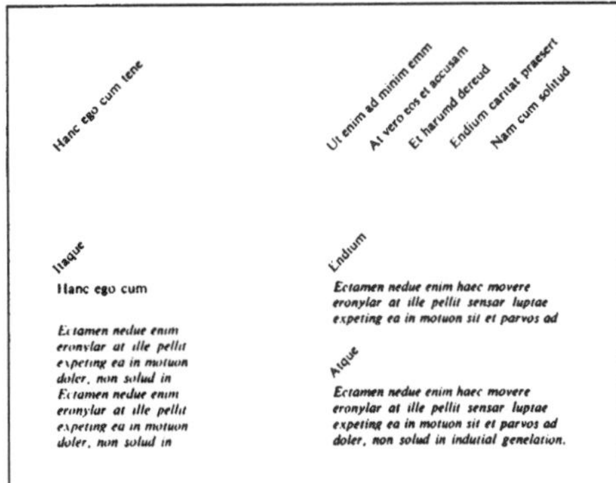


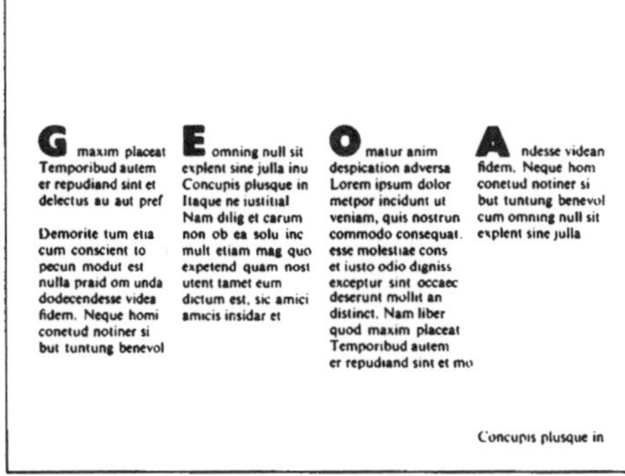

Akdfh

Lorem ipsum dolor
tempor incidunt
veniam, quis nostrund

Eawoc

Romv

Yogbcydktc

Gaoint arlglw

Hwyup qwrhc

Wehfk adyj

Romv idfb nlwg

Ccudr hikb dacns

M

Akdfh tkowhd

Eawoc falh

Ccudr hikb dacns

# Resume Grids

Grids can help to organize data on the resume. Try using them as a tool to help suggest layout positions on your blank page. Grids provide a skeletal structure for type, photos, and illustrations. Grids separate information to enhance readability. Your resume achieves a disciplined, cohesive look when grid layout is applied. Since grids reduce the number of decision points on the page, they will speed your layout decisions. Grids help answer the question, "Where do I place information on the resume?"

For maximum design flexibility, structure your resume data in narrow columns. If the resume orients vertically, three or four columns will provide more layout potential than one or two columns. Narrow columns and smaller body type help to conserve precious open space in your layout. Conversely, wide columns and large body type demand more of the page.

Consider orienting your resume horizontally. While not common, this position allows five, six, or even seven column grids for layout. Horizontal resumes comfortably accommodate the short information blocks typical of entry-level resumes.

When designing your resume grid, use the pica measure (six picas make an inch). Type lines are measured in picas, which are much easier to work with than fractional inches. Lay out margins, column widths, and alleys in whole or half picas. To retain accuracy, never mix inch and pica measures on the grid.

A strong reason for adopting grids is to impress employers with the organization of your resume. They need to feel comfortable with the information you are presenting. They must scan your data quickly, picking out and digesting the important parts. Grids enhance perceptual comfort. If you use too few grid units, however, your audience will not perceive the desired structure. Use too many units and the grid will resemble graph paper. Most effective resume grids with horizontal alleys, vary from nine to 36 units, with few exceptions. If you choose to work with column grids only, then three, four, five, or six units will provide effective organization.

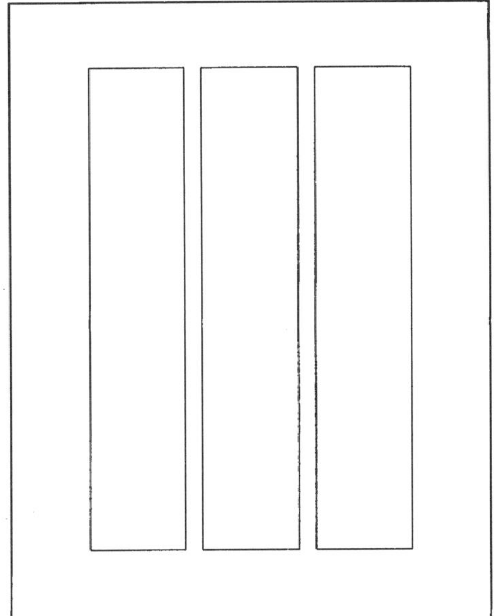

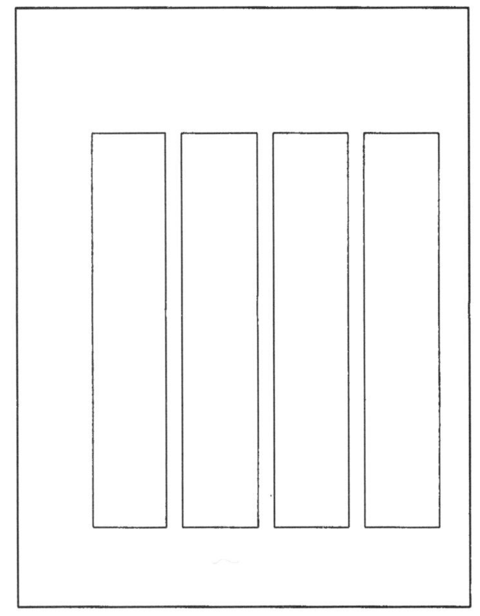

To design a logical resume grid, analyze your typeset or typewritten data. Locate the shortest subject block. Determine how many of these units will fill a single column. Plan for heads and paragraph spacing. Multiply this number by the number of columns on the page to establish a workable grid.

Page margins and alleys are arbitrary. Margins on the resume need not be uniform. Alleys may also vary. Measure both margins and alleys in picas. These external and internal spaces control the amount of "air" between resume data blocks. Narrow margins and alleys give your resume a dense look. Wide margins and alleys promote an open, flowing appearance. Use wide alleys if you wish to separate vertical type columns with a rule, line, or bar.

While rather simple to grasp by inexperienced designers, grids do not insure success. They provide logical positions for anchoring visual data, nothing more. Your designer's intuition for layout, coupled with the audience's comfort with organization makes the grid approach worthy of serious investigation.

Select the grid design approach to build proportion into your creative resume. Those templates with both horizontal and vertical alleys allow maximum fine tuning. Study tatami, golden section, Fibonacci, Mondrian, Lauwerks, and Le Corbusier proportion systems to stimulate your creative resume grid structure.

# Resume Color

Virtually all of the millions of resumes produced each year are printed in black ink on white or light-colored paper. Tradition and economy have contributed to this trend, but often these generic resume clones result from design naivety. A well-designed black and white resume will certainly function, but you should at least consider color as a personal marketing tool.

Color sensation plays a vital role in corporate identification, product recognition, and package distinction. Try proven color communication concepts to give your creative resume an edge. Pick stimulating ink colors that will evoke a positive response from employers. Choose hues that are nameable, since these will be best recognized and recalled. Beware of light tints when printing resume type. Your data must have sufficient contrast to be easily read. Pure hues have great attraction power and allow good contrast. Remember that only a few dark colors provide satisfactory printed halftone photos.

Resume ink colors should be chosen to stimulate but not offend employers. Consider their age, sex, management level, type of firm, and geographic location. A senior corporate design manager in Boston may have a different perspective on resume color than a young female art director in a Los Angeles advertising agency. Research the conventions and expectations of your target market to help decide on colors for your creative resume.

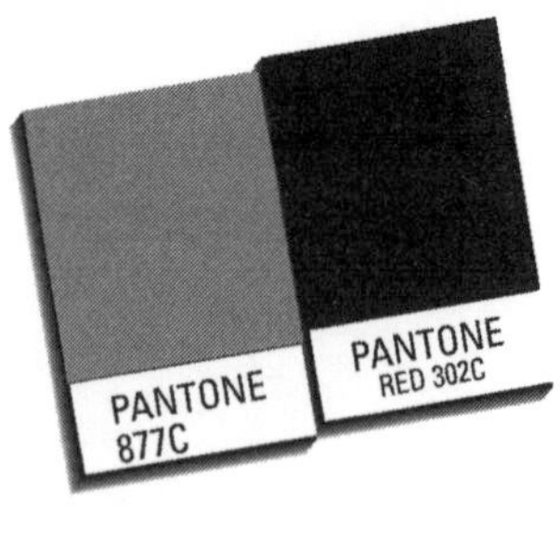

Ink colors that work well are umber, sienna, olive, the darker blues, ochre, burgundy, warm red, and both the warm and cool greys. By no means the only alternatives, these colors at least differ from the standard black, are readable when set in type, and suggest a serious document. Notice the identity colors adopted by corporations, institutions, and government agencies. Look at annual color trends for fine clothing. Consider the colors of packages with special appeal. Paint colors of exclusive automobiles might also temper your choice. Metallic gold, silver, and copper inks might build a quality association into your creative resume.

Printed varnishes can lend a subtlety to the resume. A similar effect can be achieved on the resume by screen printing, varnish, or with aerosol spray gloss media. Contrast between dull and gloss resume surfaces gives a richness that demands a doubletake. Varnish is too subtle for body type but is effective for large type and geometric shapes. Select suede finish paper to amplify the effect of varnishing.

Soft colors can be added to each resume with the airbrush at very little cost. Similar effects would be prohibitively expensive to print offset. Desktop printers can deliver a similar effect with graduated color. Complex, layered, multicolored surfaces can be produced with digital drawing and photo software.

Be specific when communicating your resume ink color to the printer. Simply to indicate a blue ink is not enough. Hundreds of distinct blues are possible. Examine the house ink chart and convey your specific color and number code in writing. Include a PMS universal color matching chip with your resume file for foolproof ink specification. The PMS mixing formulas serve as the accepted standard for designers and printers.

# Resume Photography

Photography may be appropriate for the creative resume. Your identity, samples of your work, or your resume theme might be shown in photographic form. Unique photo images may make positive lasting impressions on employers.

One of the great resume clichés is a photo of the job applicant in business attire—the kind of photo that might also appear in a university yearbook or on a graduation announcement. Surprisingly, some resumes show complete family portraits, include pets, and look as if they might double as Christmas cards. Photos of job seekers costumed as clowns, animals, and pencils might be fine for a Halloween party but hardly fit resumes. Creativity implies an appropriate level of taste.

Your photo image can be placed in context on the creative resume. Explore special-effects images. A high-contrast photo (without medium values) can take on a symbolic quality. Silhouette photos, either full or partial, lend dynamic shapes to the resume layout. Photographs altered with straight-line, mezzotint, dry brush, or etched graphic arts screens can transform a common image. Extremely coarse screens will distort your photo in a memorable way. Multiple-exposure images offer unusual potential. Special-effects photography can help plant your resume firmly in the minds of employers.

Photo impact on the resume is greater if the image is extremely large or small. Avoid wallet-sized photos, since they are commonplace. Perhaps your portrait, with resume data surprinted, might fill the resume's entire page. Small postage-stamp-sized portraits quietly register your identity with employers.

Halftone photographs on the resume demand careful handling. Select coated resume stock for superior halftones. Specify 100 line, 133 line, or 150 line halftone screens to achieve sharp images. Coarser 65 line and 85 line screens often used in newspapers give a rough image with obvious dots. Your printer or paper vendor will have on file samples of printed pieces with a wide range of halftone effects on assorted papers. Use these resources to help plan for the best use of halftones on your creative resume.

Photographers may wish to show work samples on the resume. Halftones printed on resume stock merely approach but never match the fidelity of original photographs. To avoid disappointment, use images larger than 2 x 2 inches with good value range. Plan your resume printing on a high-grade coated sheet and select a quality printer. Avoid quick-printing shops with duplicating presses. Expect to pay more for halftones on your resume, but the cost may be well worth it.

Full-color offset printing is seldom seen on resumes due to the high cost of separations and press work. The cost may be justifiable if you plan to market yourself nationally with hundreds of copies. Digital desktop printing has improved dramatically—offering high resolution color. This choice can be cost effective for 20-50 resumes.

As an alternative to printed halftones, photographs might be attached to each preprinted resume. Develop a batch of images on lightweight photo paper. Trim each print precisely to finish size with an art knife. Spray mount each print to a predetermined zone on the resume. Heavyweight resume stock will accommodate attached photos without paper distortion. This technique involves considerable hand work but guarantees photographic integrity with a fine art "feel."

# Special Effects

Creative resume design dictates that you push beyond the norm. You may want to do more than just print ink on paper. Consider altering the paper sheet to make your resume unique. Expensive die cutting can be duplicated with a few hand tools. Cut a corner off your resume sheet with a scissors. Round corners in the same manner. Cut a zig-zag edge with pinking shears. Slice a slot or simple shape through the resume with an art knife or razor blade. Punch or drill round holes in the sheets. Combine folding with die cutting to achieve a layered look.

Blind embossing by hand, a simple operation, can add sophistication to your resume. The process provides a bas-relief effect by raising part of the paper surface. With an erasing shield, paper die, or plastic drafting template and a burnisher you can raise an image. Lines, letterforms, and geometric shapes emboss easily. Complex silhouettes and multilevel forms are also possible but time-consuming.

Identification value might be added to your resume with an embossing tool like those used to identify library books and certify documents. Emboss very deep impressions on your printed resume with a binding press. Linoleum, wood, or metal plates with considerable pressure will make a lasting impression in your resume sheet. Perform your embossing experiments on selected papers before printing. Uncoated stocks with a heavy weight and high cotton content usually emboss best. Resume economics rule out machine embossing because of die and press costs. Hand techniques are effective, however, and add tactile quality to your creative resume.

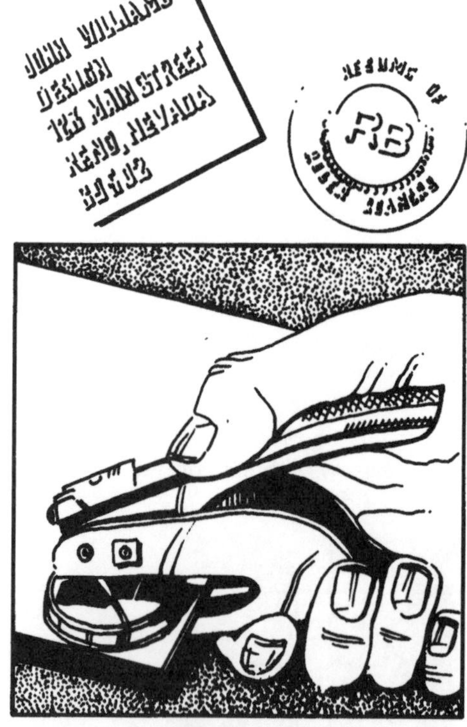

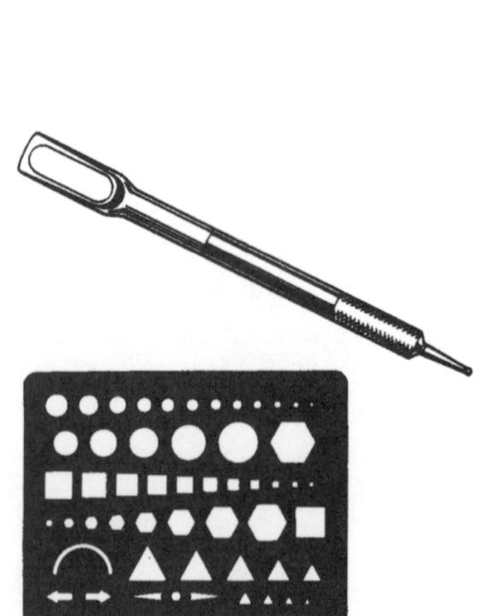

Try colorful adhesive materials to help your resume stand out. Visit any stationery store, office supplier, or paper shop for examples of adhesive seals, tags, price markers, stickers, etc. Colored dots, circles, and squares can enhance the creative resume. Vinyl letters, numbers, and arrows might reinforce your personal statement. Foil seals, stars, and tapes can add a reflective quality. Die-cut light bulbs, clouds, rainbows, or pencils might be altered or combined to anchor your resume composition. Make unique add-on shapes from paper, vinyl, or foil by hand cutting. Spray-on adhesive will provide a firm bond. Although originally created for other functions, adhesive devices offer excellent design potential. Your innovative use of stick-ons can transform an ordinary resume into a creative resume.

Rubber stamps can provide an inexpensive form of hand printing on your resume. Long used on envelopes and packages, rubber stamping is quite common on correspondence, business cards, and labels. Printmakers even use rubber stamps as a fine-arts tool.

Rubber stamps typically print a rather filmy image with rough edges. This stencil-like appearance offers sharp contrast to the precision of resume body type. Rubber stamps add an obvious handmade character to your resume in black or colored ink.

Rubber stamps are widely available in hundreds of design motifs. Custom stamps can be prepared from your simple art at a moderate price. If you design your rubber stamp, plan bold lines and shapes. Fine detail tends to spread and smudge. An artist's resume might include an original signed artwork on each copy. Woodblock, screen print, or linoleum block editions can be produced after resume printing. Combining two printing processes is tricky, and paper selection is critical. Yet this creative resume can have high impact and will probably be saved by the employer.

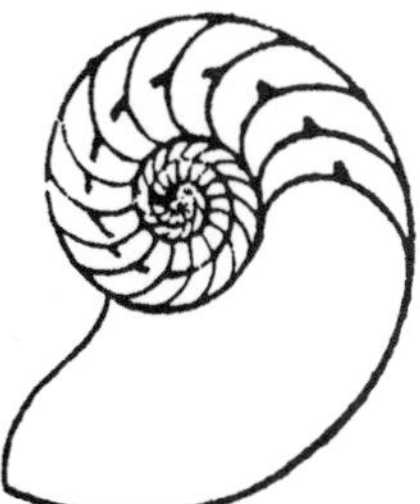

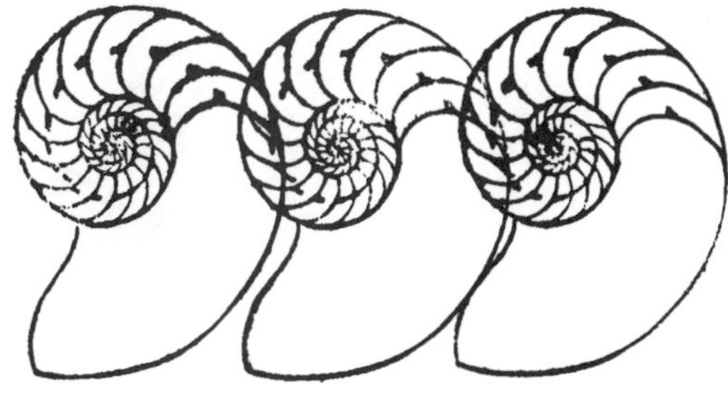

# Resume Paper

Paper sets the creative resume in context. Resume paper selections are often made casually and later regretted. Employers are sensitive to the visual and tactile qualities of resume sheets. Fine-quality paper with good snap and an elegant finish seldom fails to make a positive impression. All efforts in designing a successful resume are diluted by a naive paper selection.

Weigh several factors when selecting paper for your creative resume. If you purchase 100 or so standard-sized resumes, paper costs will not vary greatly whether bond, text, or cover grade. You will pay a bit more for heavyweight stock, but not much, providing you select a house or stocked sheet. Special-order papers will be much more expensive, perhaps prohibitively so. Always inquire about house paper inventories at your printer. Chances are that several excellent resume papers will be available as overage from previous jobs, at a good price. This is particularly important when your paper selection is a coated stock or your design requires printed bleeds.

Paper color is your first consideration. Steer clear of brightly colored sheets. Poor contrast between type and some paper colors erodes readability. Gaudy resumes may stand out in a stack, but also carry the stigma of cheap flyers and handouts. If your design concept requires a surface color, print white paper with a full bleed reverse. Printing the entire sheet produces white type. Or overprint the inked surface with dark type to gain a three-color look for the price of two colors.

Select white, ivory, beige, tan, or gray paper for the creative resume. Recycled sheets can present an environment-friendly look with subtle flecked finishes. You will seldom go wrong with these classic colors. They afford good contrast with dark type and connote professionalism. Paper colors other than white will affect any colored inks printed on them. To insure your resume color concept remains intact through printing, consult your printer. Examine sample books showing printed inks (and screens) on colored stock. Be careful when combining gray, tan, or beige paper with colored inks. Printed results often provide an unpleasant surprise.

Paper surface makes a tactile impression on the employer. A resume that feels good to the touch helps reflect your attention to detail and appreciation of quality. Smoother, coated sheets accept finer halftone screens, allow more precise type edges, and assure greater color fidelity than do uncoated papers. Coated papers are available in finishes that range from suede to glossy. Uncoated papers vary from smooth to quite rough. Rougher surfaces demonstrate an embossed quality, absorb light, and are described as having laid, wove, linen, tweed, pebble, cockle, antique, eggshell, and vellum finishes.

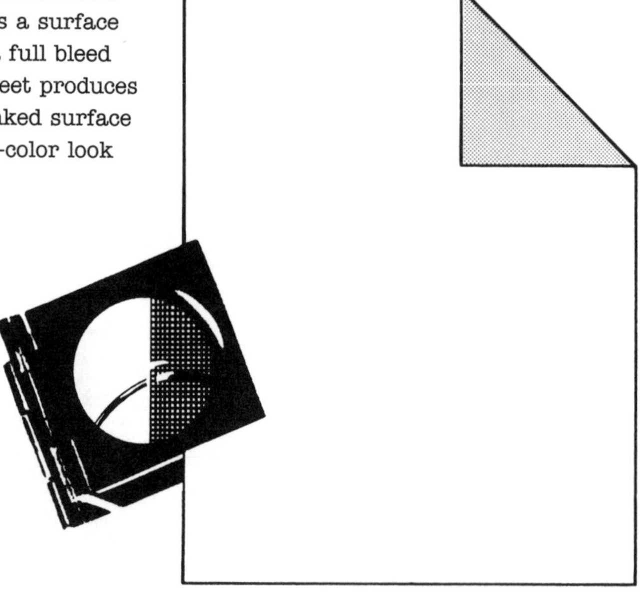

Uncoated paper makes a mature, classic statement often associated with corporate stationery, documents, currency, and books. Coated paper visually relates to brochures, annual reports, magazines, and packages. Vellum sheets have a smooth translucent quality suggestive of architectural or engineering applications. Gather samples of several surface types before you make a final selection. Your printer will have house stocks in each category to recommend. Consider the entire range of paper surfaces to stage your creative resume.

Paper weight relates to how thick your resume feels, how it folds, and how it is classified. Bond, book, text, and cover papers vary in order from light to heavy weight. Most resumes are printed on bond, but book, text, and cover stocks also work well. If your resume requires folding, bond is a wise choice. The other grades should be scored by machine or hand to fold crisply. Select a 24 or 28 pound bond for superior opacity. Bond sheets with an 80% or 100% cotton content tend to elevate your resume above the business norm and give the "snap" of quality.

Printing your resume on heavier text or cover stock has certain advantages. The document feels weighty and important. Heavier stocks emboss and die-cut more effectively. You have the opportunity to print business cards and thank you cards on the same press sheet. The heavier resume can be mailed in a large envelope without folding. Storage is no problem, since resumes are normally stored unfolded.

Select smooth surface (coated) paper when laser printing your resume. This will insure maximum edge sharpness for type, symbols, and photos. Rough textured sheets compromise image quality.

Consider some unusual uses of paper for the resume. A deckle (ragged) edge on the top or bottom of the resume sheet can lend a warm touch. Grid paper, ledger paper, parchment, and drafting vellum have resume potential. Some unusual translucent and transparent plastic films may fit your needs. Duplex stocks, with different colors front and back give a high quality impression. After printing your resume, laminate another colored sheet to it with spray adhesive to make a unique duplex. Consider printing the back of your resume with another color or complementary pattern. Specify a mixed stack (several colors of the same stock) on your press run. Some of the varied resumes may prove to be outstanding.

You may decide to conduct your job search with matching resumes, cover letters, envelopes, business cards, and thank you cards. Choose a paper system with identical color and finish in bond, text, and cover weights. Or select papers with subtle color differences but similar finishes to build a family relationship.

Remember that the two sides of a sheet of paper differ in quality. Check to see that your resume has been printed on the proper side. If not, reject the job. An employer will notice. Be sure to indicate any folding requirement to the printer so that the grain direction of the sheet will be adjusted before the press run.

| *Bond Papers* | *Coated Offset Papers* | *Uncoated Offset Papers* | *Text/Cover Papers* |
|---|---|---|---|
| ***Classic Laid*** | ***Black & White*** | ***Beckett Expressive*** | ***Americana*** |
| ***Cranes Crest*** | ***Karma*** | ***Carnival Kraft*** | ***Cambric*** |
| ***Gilbert*** | ***Kromekote*** | ***Glama Clear*** | ***Crown Graphika*** |
| ***Kilmory*** | ***Patina*** | ***French Speckletone*** | ***Gainsborough*** |
| ***Neenah*** | ***Vintage*** | ***Pegasus Quest*** | ***Skytone*** |
| ***Strathmore Writing*** | ***Quintessence*** | ***Graphika!*** | ***Starwhite*** |

# Handlettered Resume

Handlettering can include very functional architectural, engineering, or cartographic styles. It can also extend through your personal handwriting to historic, decorative, and experimental calligraphy.

The handlettered resume should only be attempted if your skills are exceptional. Poorly executed lettering will subtract from the power of your creative resume.

Handlettering is intensely personal, and at its finest demonstrates detail, discipline, and control. Creative directors place high value on fine books, historical documents, maps, certificates, and show awards. With careful craft your creative resume might become a similar treasure.

HANDLETTERFONT
HANDLETTERFONT
HANDLETTERFONT
Handletterfont
Handletterfont

The power of handlettering is demonstrated by the famous signatures of John Hancock, Frank Lloyd Wright, Picasso, and others. Your identity and resume titles might contrast lettering with precise typography. A complete handlettered resume is more of a challenge but has potential. Research graphic samples by Deaver, Girvin, Goines, Stermer, Walton, Waters, and Zapf for inspiration.

Experiment with pencils, steel pens, fountain pens, quills, and brush pens to create letterfonts that are unique, consistent, and elegant. Above all your handlettered resume must be readable. If you confuse the reader with ornate, complex, frilly, or mis-scaled letterforms, don't count on a thorough review of your resume contents.

darold heikens

EXPERIENCE

MANAGER 1982-PRESENT
GRAD II RESTAURANTS INC.
SAN LUIS OBISPO, CA.

ENVIROMENTAL DESIGN 1978-82
MJP INC.
FORT COLLINS, CO.

LANDSCAPE ARCHITECT 1981
EAST CENTRAL COUNCIL OF GOVERNMENTS
BURLINGTON, CO.

AUDIO-VISUAL PRODUCTION 1980
U.S. FOREST SERVICE
DENVER, CO.

SELF EMPLOYED DESIGNER
ALTERED ESTATES
FORT COLLINS, CO.
CHICO, CA.

EDUCATION

B.A. LANDSCAPE ARCHITECTURE
COLORADO STATE UNIVERSITY
FORT COLLINS, CO.

VISUAL COMMUNICATIONS
CALIFORNIA STATE UNIVERSITY
CHICO, CA.

PERSONAL

DAROLD "DODGER" HEIKENS
1565 N. CHERRY ST.
CHICO, CA. 95926
(916) 891-5732
BIRTHDATE 2/05/'59
SINGLE PARENT

# Typewritten Resume

Until 1980, typewritten resumes were the professional norm. Today this low-tech process might still be appropriate if you are a writer, editor, or want to project a retro impression.

With ingenuity you can avoid the generic look of the typewriter. Both the larger Pica (10 characters per inch) and smaller Elite (12 characters per inch) sizes are functional. Pica fonts afford greater legibility. Elite fonts more closely resemble digital typesetting and feature tighter letterspacing.

If you decide to typewrite, clean the keys, ball, or wheel. Invest in a new carbon ribbon. A second backing sheet in the typewriter will help provide sharper impressions. Type on bright white 25% bond paper for crisp edge originals.

Electric typewriters are preferable to manual machines. Electrics deliver uniform striking pressures and more precise characters. If your typewritten original lacks sharpness, photocopy or scan it to add density to the typewritten characters.

Design to the strength of typewritten characters. Ragged right setting (what you are now reading) is appropriate. Enlarge headlines, exaggerate letterspacing, or reverse the text (white letters) to lend a fresh look.

Try mixing typewritten body copy with typeset headlines. Or experiment with typewritten headlines (rough edges) as a contrast to typeset body (smooth edges). Combining processes may lead to a distinctive creative resume.

| | |
|---|---|
| **Courier 12** | ABCDEFGHIJKLMNOPQRSTUVWXYZ!°#$%/&*()_+<br>abcdefghijklmnopqrstuvwxyz1234567890-= |
| **Courier 10** | ABCDEFGHIJKLMNOPQRSTUVWXYZ°!@#$%¢&*()_+<br>abcdefghijklmnopqrstuvwxyz±1234567890-= |
| **Delegate** | ABCDEFGHIJKLMNOPQRSTUVWXYZ°!@#$%¢&*()_+<br>abcdefghijklmnopqrstuvwxyz±1234567890-= |
| **Elite** | ABCDEFGHIJKLMNOPQRSTUVWXYZ°!@#$%¢&*()_+<br>abcdefghijklmnopqrstuvwxyz±1234567890-= |
| **Letter Gothic** | ABCDEFGHIJKLMNOPQRSTUVWXYZ°!@#$%¢&*()_+<br>abcdefghijklmnopqrstuvwxyz±1234567890-= |
| **Pica** | ABCDEFGHIJKLMNOPQRSTUVWXYZ°!@#$%¢&*()_+<br>abcdefghijklmnopqrstuvwxyz±1234567890-= |

# Typeset Resume

A decision to typeset the resume shows employers a dimension of your visual taste. Typesetting implies that you managed the total production of your resume and it indicates your mastery of a particular page-layout software program. Employers assume that you selected the resume paper and approved the print quality. These valuable skills equate with those you might perform on the job.

Your opportunity to impress an employer with a typeset resume is great, so design with restraint and a sense of appropriateness. Envision an empathy with employers. See yourself in their place. Try to visualize how your typeset creative resume might impress the interviewer.

Quality typesetting is identified by its optical superiority. The decisions that you make on-screen shape both sophisticated letterspacing and appropriate linespacing for your resume. The nuances of your typography add scale and finish detail. Quality typesetting will raise your creative resume above the ordinary.

The type you select for your resume is an expression of your personal preference. Your choice will probably be based on typographic treatments you have noticed in ads, brochures, annual reports, magazines, or other resumes (such as the samples included in this book). Pay particular attention to your selection of body type, since this makes up the bulk of resume information. Remember that most body typefaces will function as headlines, but the reverse is not true.

Your creative resume should be both legible and readable. Legibility is produced by the typeface you select and results from the visual shape of individual type characters. Readability is a measure of how easy an entire page is to read. It depends on the type arrangement or composition you design. Be concerned with both factors as you create your resume.

Avant Garde
ABCDEFGHIJKLMNOPQRSTUVWXYZ abcdefghijklmnopqrstuvwxyz

Bodoni
ABCDEFGHIJKLMNOPQRSTUVWXYZ abcdefghijklmnopqrstuvwxyz

Century
ABCDEFGHIJKLMNOPQRSTUVWXYZ abcdefghijklmnopqrstuvwxyz

Eras
ABCDEFGHIJKLMNOPQRSTUVWXYZ abcdefghijklmnopqrstuvwxyz

Garamond
ABCDEFGHIJKLMNOPQRSTUVWXYZ abcdefghijklmnopqrstuvwxyz

Helvetica
ABCDEFGHIJKLMNOPQRSTUVWXYZ abcdefghijklmnopqrstuvwxyz

Optima
ABCDEFGHIJKLMNOPQRSTUVWXYZ abcdefghijklmnopqrstuvwxyz

**Palatino**
**ABCDEFGHIJKLMNOPQRSTUVWXYZ abcdefghijklmnopqrstuvwxyz**

Times Roman
ABCDEFGHIJKLMNOPQRSTUVWXYZ abcdefghijklmnopqrstuvwxyz

Base your choice of typeface partly on its availability in a variety of weights and in an italic version. A large type family like Helvetica, Univers, Times Roman, or Garamond allows you great design potential without changing typefaces. If you must use more than one typeface for your resume, practice restraint. One or two additional typefaces can be effective, but a single choice is preferable. After all, the resume is a rather simple visual statement. Too many typefaces will compete with each other and detract from the "Big Idea" of your creative resume.

Pick a typeface with a visual personality that appeals to you. Your choice must enhance the resume message and stimulate the employer. Whether your selection is serif or sans serif is not important. Depend on the time-tested type classics to deliver a positive response.

Organize your resume information into a cohesive typographic structure. Ragged-right setting is best. Ragged-left is sometimes effective if you plan short, discrete information blocks. Avoid justified setting, which can involve erratic word-spacing. Minimize hyphenation and edit carefully for "widows" (single words at ends of blocks, starts of new pages or columns).

Plan adequate 1- or 2-point linespacing for your body information. Paragraphs will appear crowded and difficult to read without careful linespacing. Negative linespacing packs paragraphs even more tightly. Linespacing of 3-, 4- points, or more spreads copy, quiets your message but may consume excessive page space.

Cap/lowercase typesetting is comfortable to read and is recommended. Avoid all-lowercase composition. All caps typesetting is possible with a few typefaces, but this choice will retard reading speed by at least 15%. Most employers feel at ease reading 8-, 9-, and 10-point body type. Selections smaller than 8-point should be made with extreme caution. You risk offending employers if they must squint or use a magnifier to read your resume.

Garamond Light
ABCDEFGHIJKLMnopqrstuvwxyz

*Garamond Light Italic*
*ABCDEFGHIJKLMnopqrstuvwxyz*

Garamond Book
ABCDEFGHIJKLMnopqrstuvwxyz

***Garamond Book Italic***
***ABCDEFGHIJKLMnopqrstuvwxyz***

Garamond Book Condensed
ABCDEFGHIJKLMnopqrstuvwxyz

*Garamond Book Condensed Italic*
*ABCDEFGHIJKLMnopqrstuvwxyz*

**Garamond Bold**
**ABCDEFGHIJKLMnopqrstuvwxyz**

***Garamond Bold Italic***
***ABCDEFGHIJKLMnopqrstuvwxyz***

Helvetica Light
ABCDEFGHIJKLMnopqrstuvwxyz

*Helvetica Light Italic*
*ABCDEFGHIJKLMnopqrstuvwxyz*

Helvetica Regular
ABCDEFGHIJKLMnopqrstuvwxyz

*Helvetica Regular Italic*
*ABCDEFGHIJKLMnopqrstuvwxyz*

**Helvetica Bold**
**ABCDEFGHIJKLMnopqrstuvwxyz**

***Helvetica Bold Italic***
***ABCDEFGHIJKLMnopqrstuvwxyz***

**Helvetica Black**
**ABCDEFGHIJKLMnopqrstuvwxyz**

***Helvetica Black Italic***
***ABCDEFGHIJKLMnopqrstuvwxyz***

Critical parts of the resume deserve typographic emphasis. Your name, telephone number, and information category heads may rate special attention. Typographic emphasis is a visual signal involving contrast of position, size, weight, capitalization, italics, or color. Select only a single contrast or signal for an effective result. If you use many forms of emphasis on a single page you will build visual contradictions. Too many emphasis signals fight each other and decrease rather than enhance readability. Typographic restraint is the hallmark of the creative resume.

For headline size contrast, specify unit increments of the body type size. Notice how 12- and 18-point heads contrast nicely with 9-point body, while 12-, 16-, 20-, and 24-point heads complement 8-point body. Heads and body with only a point or two size difference appear indecisive. Build on multiples of 3 or 4 points for adequate size-scale contrast.

If your type idea involves weight change, consider jumping a weight for emphasis. For example, design with Garamond Light and Garamond Ultra, omitting standard Garamond Book. Pair Helvetica Light with Helvetica Bold, omitting Helvetica Medium. The resulting exaggeration will be effective without requiring a size or color change.

Contrast also plays a critical role if you decide to mix typefaces on the creative resume. Make sure your type styles are visually distinct. Universe and Helvetica are uncomfortable together, as are Bodoni and Palatino. In both instances the pairs are visually similar and lack contrast. However, Garamond Italic and Helvetica Bold are compatible because they show obvious contrast.

---

**Emphasis**

**Typographic emphasis is a visual signal involving contrast of size, weight, capitalization or italics.**

---

# Emphasis

**Typographic emphasis is a visual signal involving contrast of size, weight, capitalization or italics.**

---

**Emphasis**

**Typographic emphasis is a visual signal involving contrast of size, weight, capitalization or italics.**

---

## Emphasis

**Typographic emphasis is a visual signal involving contrast of size, weight, capitalization or italics.**

---

# Emphasis

**Typographic emphasis is a visual signal involving contrast of size, weight, capitalization or italics.**

---

*Contrast*

Select a single visual signal to provide a typographic emphasis and enhance resume readability.

---

CONTRAST

Select a single visual signal to provide typographic emphasis and enhance resume readability.

---

**Contrast**

Select a single visual signal to provide typographic emphasis and enhance resume readability.

---

***Contrast***

***Select a single visual signal to provide typographic emphasis and enhance resume readability.***

---

Drop initials set into body type combine with indentation to give a strong visual signal which provides typographic emphasis.

---

Paragraphing the creative resume is another factor to consider. When in doubt, specify at least one linespace between paragraphs. This style provides type blocks that are easy to scan and eliminates the need to indent. If you prefer an indented look, be bold about it. The most common indent is one-em, but a two-em space also works well. Specify "hanging" quotations to help preserve strong paragraph margins.

Consider these hints for your creative resume. Notice how borders reduce the size of the resume page and are usually decorative rather than functional. Eliminate subheads for more direct communication. Emphasis bullets are a resume cliché but have real potential if used with elegance. Pay particular attention to punctuation marks in the type font you select. Innovative use of periods, commas, dashes, colons, and slashes can lend sophistication to your type concept and enhance readability. Display initials are seldom seen in resumes but can add welcome contrast within paragraphs if you select an editorial style. Explore the resume potential of leaders (dotted lines) as an alternative to lines (rules).

Final resume typographic decisions will reflect your level of visual sensitivity. Where you place resume data on the page is important. Outstanding layouts have common structural qualities. The unprinted parts of your resume page should be dynamic and flowing. Guard this precious white space. Preserve as much of it as possible to showcase your resume data. Controlled contrast should be obvious in your typography.

Your layout should relate to reading patterns: left to right, top to bottom, start to finish. Pay particular attention to page margins and corners as you strive for a dynamic balance of elements. Develop an asymmetrical design, built on a solid type structure. Depend on your clear typographic concept to give positive signals to employers. Keep typographic excess out of the way of the resume message to help make your creative resume successful.

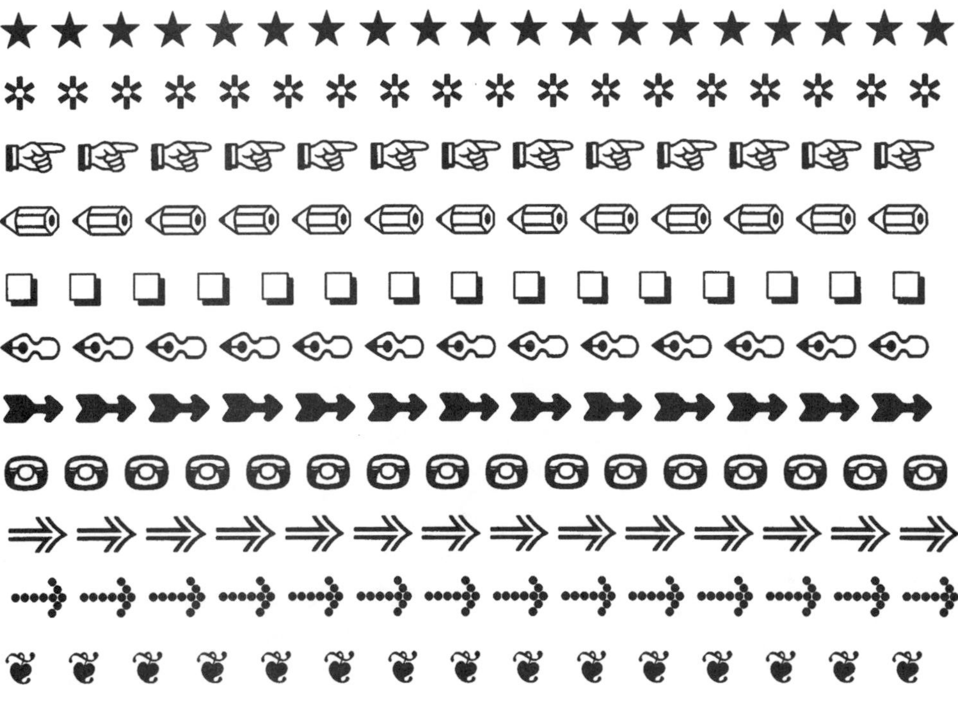

# Branded Resume

Ideation for your creative resume might build on current theory for branding products and organizations. Your document should exude both tangible and intangible qualities. With your resume you project actual type, color, paper, and pictorial dynamics. Yet you can promise more! By branding yourself you can imprint reviewers and resonate the intangibles of "classy," "worldly," "savvy," "articulate," or "cool" that you possess.

Branding relates to reputation, esteem, relevance, and most important—differentiation. These are all positive attributes your might project. Consider the brand power of Apple, Nike, Levi's, Pepsi, Sony, and other renowned products. While your creative resume will hardly make you a household name—only frequent exposure over time will do that; clever branding will help you stand above the crowd.

Your name itself may be a hidden treasure. Tamara Whiteside branded her resume by printing her name on a folded duplex sheet revealing a white band down the left edge. Sara Waters created a "wet" resume by flowing varnish over her vertical name. Patricia Chikasawa branded her resume by integrating pronunciation marks with her tongue-twisting family name—changing a liability into a visual asset. What might you create with the name Springfield, Blackburn, Roundtree, Thornberry, or Westlake?

Type, well chosen, has proven branding potential. Style selections can project gender, elegance, technical, formal, romantic, and cutting-edge positions. Smart type choices create value beyond personal preferences and help stake out a unique visual stance for your creative resume.

Consider the creative branding power of the rebus. Milton Glaser's I ♥ NY and Paul Rand's buzzing IBM are imprinted on the brain of every serious designer. Perhaps your first, middle, last, or nickname has similar potential.

Reflecting exceptional physical appearance might help launch your creative concept. Extreme height might suggest a tall or vertical fold format. Red hair might be reinforced with red ink or paper. Distinctive blue eyes might be projected with metallic ink. Your perfect smile might connect by choosing ultra-white stock for your creative resume.

Branding can be reinforced by extending your unique resume identity to all collateral in your job search kit. Project your brand on website, fax, letterhead, mailing label, business card, thank-you cards, and reminder mailers to build recognition through a consistent system.

# Resume Systems

You will certainly benefit by adopting a systems approach to your resume. By extending your unique identity to a variety of applications you can clearly demonstrate a mastery of the visual linking of various sizes and shapes of collateral. This important skill adds value to your professional preparation.

A systems approach is often used by publication designers to bring unity to brochures, annual reports, maps, travel guides, tickets etc.—when multiple variations on a theme are appropriate. Effective systems design minimizes contradiction. It extends typographic style, scale and perhaps a grid structure to each application. Color and paper selections are matched or chosen as part of a total palette. Margins are metered to build in proportional consistency.

Designers often adopt a systems approach for economy. A well chosen paper stock will work in different weights and save money. By ganging many graphic pieces on a large press sheet, printing costs can be shaved. Careful planning might allow you to print simultaneously on a higher quality press.

Designers with a thorough command of layout systems are always in demand to interpret and present complex information for both print and screen. Take advantage of your creative resume and follow-up pieces to showcase your systems design expertise.

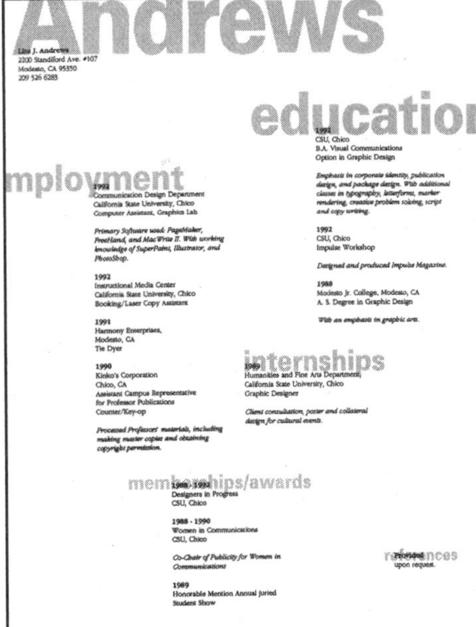
Andrews

Lisa J. Andrews
2200 Standiford Ave. #107
Modesto, CA 95350
209 526 6283

educatio

1992
CSU, Chico
B.A. Visual Communications
Option in Graphic Design

*Emphasis in corporate identity, publication design, and package design. With additional classes in typography, letterforms, marker rendering, creative problem solving, script and copy writing.*

1992
CSU, Chico
Impulse Workshop

*Designed and produced Impulse Magazine.*

1988
Modesto Jr. College, Modesto, CA
A. S. Degree in Graphic Design

*With an emphasis in graphic arts.*

mployment

1992
Communication Design Department
California State University, Chico
Computer Assistant, Graphics Lab

*Primary Software used: PageMaker, FreeHand, and MacWrite II. With working knowledge of SuperPaint, Illustrator, and PhotoShop.*

1992
Instructional Media Center
California State University, Chico
Booking/Laser Copy Assistant

1991
Harmony Enterprises,
Modesto, CA
Tie Dyer

1990
Kinko's Corporation
Chico, CA
Assistant Campus Representative
for Professor Publications
Counter/Key-op

*Processed Professors' materials, including making master copies and obtaining copyright permission.*

internships

1989
Humanities and Fine Arts Department,
California State University, Chico
Graphic Designer

*Client consultation, poster and collateral design for cultural events.*

memberships/awards

1988 - 1992
Designers in Progress
CSU, Chico

1988 - 1990
Women in Communications
CSU, Chico

*Co-Chair of Publicity for Women in Communications*

1989
Honorable Mention Annual juried
Student Show

references

Provided
upon request.

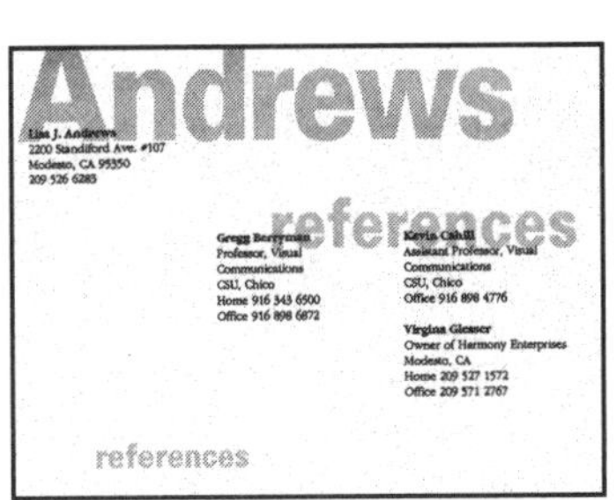
Andrews

Lisa J. Andrews
2200 Standiford Ave. #107
Modesto, CA 95350
209 526 6285

references

Gregg Berryman
Professor, Visual
Communications
CSU, Chico
Home 916 343 6500
Office 916 898 6872

Kevin Cahill
Assistant Professor, Visual
Communications
CSU, Chico
Office 916 898 4776

Virgina Glesser
Owner of Harmony Enterprises
Modesto, CA
Home 209 527 1572
Office 209 571 2767

references

Andrews

Lisa J. Andrews
2200 Standiford Ave. #107
Modesto, CA 95350

designe
209 526 6285

# On-Screen Resume

Your creative resume may be shaped for the screen to be delivered on the Internet. Different from print, screen design demands both a "look" and "feel" to be browsed and explored by targeted viewers.

Consider the strength of each medium. Print is unsurpassed for subtlety and tactile surface. The printed resume begs the touch, offers smooth and rough textures, and can exude warmth. It lasts, but delivery is limited.

On-screen resumes are cool, detached, and fleeting. Yet they are readily accessible day and night with a simple click. Your on-screen resume can deliver information in a linear, hierarchical, web, parallel, matrix, overlay, or spatial zoom format. Consider the potential of each organization model to design effectively for the screen.

Focus on a format appropriate for short content. Multiple screens are not necessary. Build obvious pathways which support intuitive wayfinding. Craft your resume data so it may be effortlessly navigated by viewers.

Test your on-screen resume for user reading comfort. Plan large legible type, build an adequate contrast, and brand the screen with your distinct color and pictorial image. Minimize scrolling and layering. Like the printed resume, your screen version should be easily scanned by all interviewers.

Your on-screen resume can be a powerful tool and perfect companion for your web portfolio. If you can deliver your data with a welcome "feel," your creative resume can extend the range of your job search.

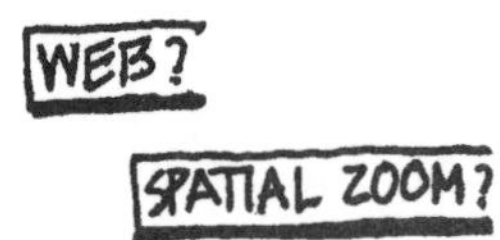


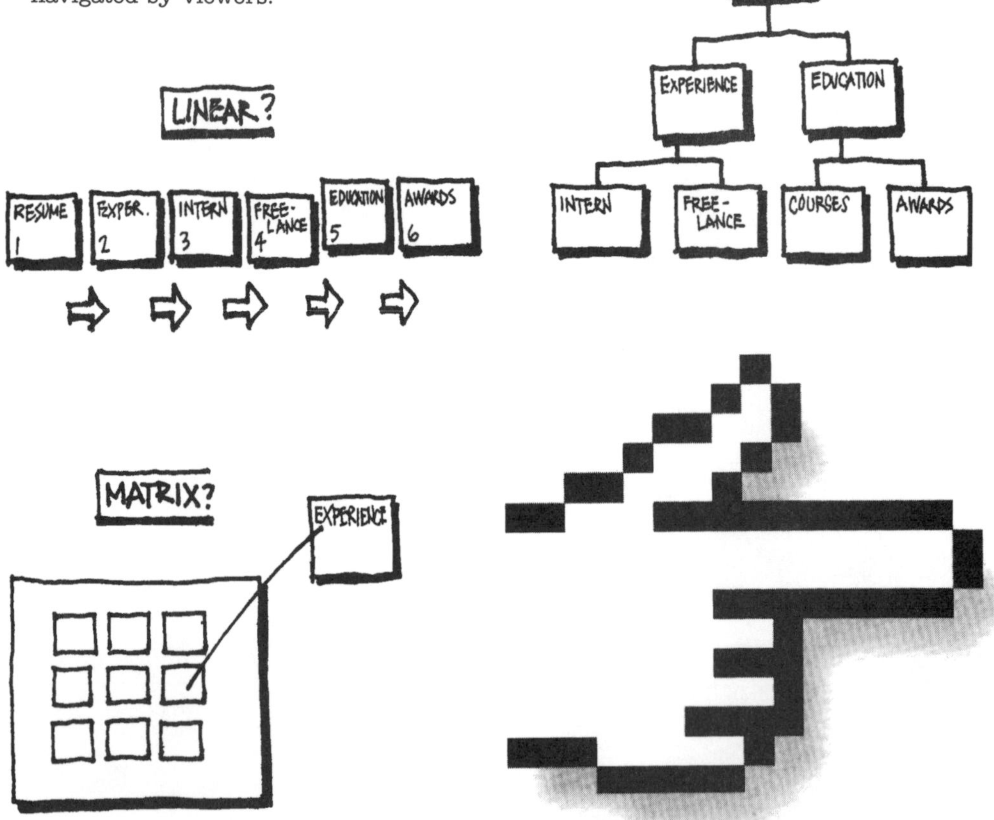

# Multiplatform Resume

Your creative resume is a document capable of being delivered effectively across multiple platforms. Consider the end user. Will it fax well? Photocopy clearly? Scan into a database? How will it appear on screen if delivered from a floppy, Zip disc, CD-ROM, videodisc, as an e-mail or web image? Might your creative resume be transmitted via pager, cell phone, or personal organizer?

Think globally to link across platforms. If you design with the reader foremost in mind, delivery systems become more seamless and transparent. Shape your resume content to neutralize the specific delivery technology.

Develop a powerful systems approach through rational information hierarchy, legible typography, consistent layout, strong branding, and distinctive color. The effective multiplatform resume will reveal your careful planning to sophisticated reviewers.

Some danger lurks with the total multiplatform resume. By serving all available technologies you may dilute the impact of your resume. You can ill afford a generic personal document. If your resume becomes a common black and white page with 16-point Times type to function on all platforms then you have missed this target.

Narrow your choice of platforms to those most likely to be used by your interviewer. Thoroughly test the result in each application before launching your creative resume.

# Printing Alternatives

How many resume copies will you need? One hundred is a good target number. When in doubt, order more, not fewer. If you plan a major mailing, several hundred might be appropriate. So what if you get your target job and use only a few resumes? This small investment in your future will certainly be amortized. Remember that resume typesetting, printing, and mailing costs (plus other job-search expenses) are tax deductible.

Consider the photocopy process for duplicating your resume. Great strides have been made in the technology of this process. Sharp dense type and images are now the norm. Shop around to locate a machine capable of clean, precise reproductions. Duplicate your resume at a high-end service bureau or at the local photocopy shop, since new machines produce superior copies. Machines in libraries, bookstores, and supermarkets tend to be heavily used, casually maintained, and often deliver inferior photocopies.

Many resumes are printed on offset duplicators, sheet-fed machines found in instant print shops throughout the country. Capable of fast, inexpensive, good-quality printing, these small machines handle 8-1/2 x 11 inch resume sheets with ease. Best for single-color resumes, an offset duplicator in the hands of a skilled operator is capable of multi-color imaging with fair registration.

Avoid the "quick-print" process if your resume design demands large ink blocks, reverse areas, and full bleeds. Precision registration of two or more colors is not recommended on duplicators. Very fine lines and small type can also pose serious problems. Offset duplication is satisfactory for most resume reproduction if you design within the limits of the machine. If you ask more than is possible with this equipment, expect a level of quality below that necessary for your creative resume.

Resumes that require precise registration and printing of superior quality should be directed to shops with offset presses. This step up from offset duplicators is usually more expensive but worth it. Sheet-fed offset lithography presses with high-quality plates can reproduce very sophisticated images. Expect fine detail, consistent ink coverage, and precise halftones. Often these presses print two colors on the same pass for additional precision. Since larger paper sizes are usually run on offset presses, consider printing business cards, reference cards, and thank-you cards on the same press sheet with your resume. Employers are used to handling fine printing in the form of brochures, catalogs, sales literature, posters, and annual reports. Fine quality printing helps your creative resume communicate with employers in their language, at their high level.

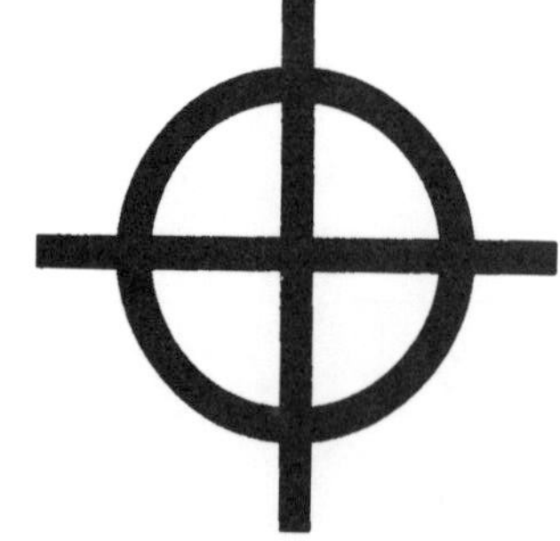

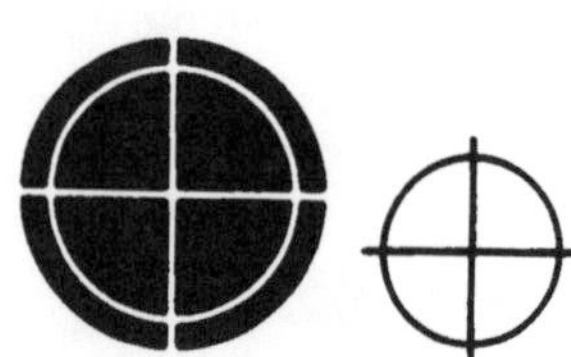

Resume printing costs range from a few dollars to several hundred dollars. Photocopy resumes are the least expensive. Duplicated resumes cost slightly more. Digital color resumes and precision offset resumes demand the highest price.

Photocopies are billed by the copy, without significant price breaks. Press runs on duplicators and offset presses feature price breaks per 50 or 100 copies. Price differences between 25 and 200 one-color resumes are insignificant, due only to paper prices. Select larger resume quantities for better value.

If your offset resume requires other than black ink, expect an additional ink change mixing charge. Two-color and three-color resumes are more costly, since they require extra negatives, plates, and press runs. Plan to pay slightly more if your resume design includes halftones, reverses, bleeds, folds, or unusual trims.

Digital color printers provide high resolution resumes directly from an electronic file. One advantage is that you can print any quantity as needed. Proofs and modifications are a snap.

Visit two or three firms to get resume printing estimates. Bring along your mock-up resume to enhance communication. Written quotations are recommended to help you avoid later misunderstandings. Don't be surprised if the estimates vary. You are shopping to save money, but a few dollars saved is false economy if it means compromising the quality and precision of your creative resume.

When you take delivery of your resumes inspect all printing carefully. Be sure that your specifications have been met. Verify resume quantity with a quick count. Printing must be on the proper side of the paper. Printed images should be accurate. Type should have sharp edges. Ink coverage and color should be consistent. Unprinted areas should be free of dust or fingerprints. Check for precise cropping. Examine the back of each resume for ink set-off (marks from the sheet below during printing) as this will depreciate your resume quality. Take a few minutes to inspect the job in the print shop, before you make payment. If the printing is sloppy, request a rerun. Quality control is your responsibility and is essential for the creative resume.

# Resume Innovations

If you really want to stand out from the crowd, consider creating an innovative resume. This direction dictates a truly unique presentation format, one that has never before been attempted. Innovative resumes require inventive skills that are rare even among creative people. On a high plane, innovative resumes can be extremely effective. They can make a powerful, unforgettable impression and virtually guarantee an interview. On the other hand, if you miss the mark your result can be a tacky dud.

The innovative approach carries with it considerable risk. Your offbeat resume must demonstrate genius and still function at a high professional level. It must marry your concept with communication. You need to target a level of appropriateness. Successful innovation requires you to feel an empathy with employers. Imagine yourself behind their desk as they receive your resume package. Forecast whether you would toss it in the trash bin or immediately reach for the telephone to schedule an interview.

Innovative resumes can startle, surprise, or challenge an employer. They might project whimsy or humor. Inventive resumes can appeal to all the senses and leave an indelible impression. They can make the day seem a little brighter while selling your unique talents. If the employer smiles after reading your innovative resume and is left with the feeling "Why didn't I think of that?", then you have hit the bull's eye.

Resume innovation completely involves your creative process. Initial ideation should flow without restraint. Proceed as you would if brainstorming. Develop lots of ideas. Record all of them in sketch form, rejecting no concept as too bizarre or outlandish. Focus on form rather than content. The resume must still contain basic data, but your innovative form will present your boilerplate resume in an unexpected manner.

Resume innovations may arrive in a flash or be the result of deliberate methodology. To enhance your chance of success develop a wide range of ideas. Give them time to incubate, then select and refine the most promising. Pre-test your innovative resume mock-up on teachers and design peers to verify its appropriateness.

One approach might be to visualize your resume as expandable. Folded down to 2 x 3-1/2 inches it might double as a business card and fit the standard filing systems for cards. Unfolded it would fit letter folders. Perhaps your resume could fold to 8-1/2 x 11 inches but expand to an 11 x 17, 11 x 34, or 17 x 22 inch poster showing samples of your work.

Maybe your resume could be an actual file folder complete with a die-cut name tab. The folder might insure your position in the records of target employers. It could hold your cover letter and other correspondence. A miniature resume might be die cut to fit rolladex address files, a practice common with business cards. Success would depend on condensing resume data and might involve printing multiple cards.

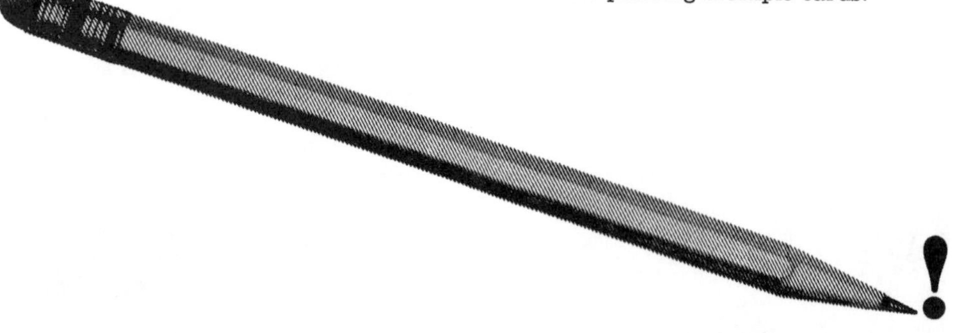

Consider designing your resume as a folding package completely die cut and scored, ready for the employer to assemble. Plan your paper structure to eliminate the need for tape or glue. Keep any verbal instructions simple. Plan for quick and easy assembly to encourage busy employers to participate in the do-it-yourself process. A wide array of three-dimensional forms is possible, ranging from representational to abstract. Folded paper airplanes might stimulate thinking in this direction. The Japanese origami tradition of paper folding suggests the considerable potential of such resume structures.

The act of opening an interesting package can be as fascinating to an executive as it is to a child at Christmas. Your innovative resume might be printed on the inside of a handmade box or bag so that opening reveals the document. Consider canning each resume on gift-wrap equipment made for that purpose. Seal your resume in shrinkwrap or vacuum-form a bubble for it. Bag it in flexible vinyl. Ship it in a sleeve package as you would a disc. Bottle it in a transparent plastic bottle or jar. Visit mailing supply stores or your post office to consider available shipping tubes, bags, envelopes, and boxes. Explore industrial packaging companies in your area to discover further possibilities. Inventive packaging with novel opening systems offers a wealth of untapped potential for the innovative resume.

Direct mail experts use premium gifts to make promotional and sales literature more memorable. Transfer this concept to your job search. Consider packaging a well-designed tool of the trade with your innovative resume. Items like push pins, pencils, and pen points are inexpensive and quite beautiful. Write a lead-in sentence in your cover letter to relate the object to your job search.

A fresh flower, an apple, a pretzel, a fortune cookie, or a wrapped piece of premium candy might increase the impact of your resume. A beautiful postage stamp, foreign coin, or fishing fly can also help reflect your level of personal taste. Collectible signed prints or photographs produced by you will keep your name in front of an employer over an extended period. Balloons, stickers, decals, buttons, and bookmarks offer short-term exposure when linked with your innovative resume. Explore stationers, hardware stores, art supply shops, and surplus outlets to locate economical items of functional simplicity.

Try to relate this approach to a specific position. If you seek a packaging job, mail your resume with an uncooked egg, a common light bulb, or a fragile wine glass to demonstrate your knowledge of container design. Test your idea thoroughly to avoid the negative association of broken glass and cracked eggshells. If you have targeted a landscape architecture position, a small package of seeds stapled to your resume might send a positive message. An exhibit designer could mail a 30 x 40 inch blueprint resume in a mailing tube. Your innovative resume should be designed in congruence with your professional target.

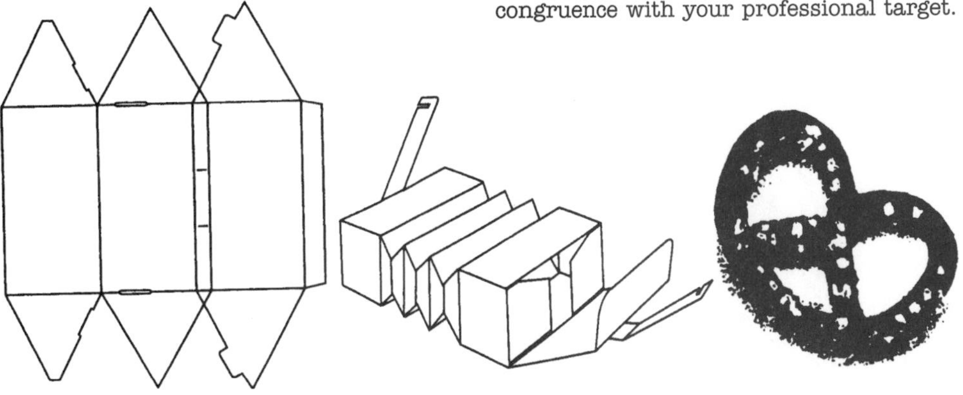

# Resume Checklist

1. Does your resume brand you as an authentic designer?
2. Are you positioned as a unique rather than generic talent?
3. Can the interviewer digest your resume with a quick scan?
4. Is your resume honed and concise—not excessive and wordy?
5. Does it challenge reviewers to read all of the document?
6. Has your resume been carefully spellchecked and edited?
7. If mailed, will your creative resume break through screening barriers?
8. Is your resume integrated with letterhead, thank you, and reference collateral?
9. Does your resume demonstrate your storytelling ability?
10. Have you fused good writing and good design?
11. Does your creative resume demonstrate impeccable typography?
12. Have you tested the resume to insure reproduction by fax or photocopy?
13. Does your creative resume predict your portfolio?
14. Will your resume function across platforms—print, fax, screen?
15. Does your creative resume stimulate an employer to want to meet you?

# Cover Letter

If you mail your resume be sure to include a cover letter. Your creative resume, no matter how well designed, remains a cool printed document. Nonspecific, it is intended to appeal to many employers. If the resume arrives in an envelope without an explanation letter, expect very limited impact.

Write a cover letter to personalize your message to an employer. Mail only to a specific individual in the organization. Include their job title. Avoid the Gentlemen, Sir, Madam, and Manager introductions so common to form letters. Never mail to the firm name only; to do so will further dilute your resume's power. Think of the cover letter as a personal introduction to the employer. Treat it as if you were describing yourself briefly on the telephone. Communicate your potential value to the firm in the cover letter. Make the employer curious enough to need to know more about you. Design your creative cover letter to generate an employer response.

Each time you mail a resume, write a unique cover letter. Perfect grammar and spelling are expected. Typesetting should be flawless. Develop a solid content structure, but personalize each letter. Steer away from the form style cover letter with mere address changes. Employers will easily spot the transparency of your effort. Photocopied cover letters are also inadequate, being mere duplicates rather than originals.

Prepare your cover letters on paper that complements your creative resume. Another approach is to select a color coordinated letterhead and envelope that tastefully contrast with your resume. White paper is always appropriate.

Adopt a proven block style business letter format. Have someone carefully proof your cover letters. Pay particular attention to spelling the name of your interview target. Sign your name neatly in a color other than black to contrast with the printed color and give your letter more visual impact. Direct mail experts have found that a dark blue signature stimulates the best reader response. Be sure to add the enclosure indication to complete the professional appearance of your creative cover letters.

**Enc:**

The creative cover letter should be short. Never exceed a single page unless you seek a writing position. Three or four economical paragraphs are adequate.

The opening paragraph is critical. Get attention with something interesting about the firm or, better yet, the reader. Be timely. Show that you are informed about the company. Mention some recent work that caught your attention. Comment on a current article by or about the employer. Compliment a professional award. Make connections between a reference, the employer, and you. Be sure to include the name, title, and organization of your reference. Mention why you are writing. Indicate here if you are responding to an advertisement or a placement tip.

Paragraph two might contain a teaser about your resume to stimulate the employer to read it thoroughly. Mention your college, degree, year, and focus if you are a recent graduate. Touch on your significant experience. Three or four sentences will be sufficent.

Use paragraph three to create a special interest in you. Connect your unique skills to the needs of an employer. Even if no position exists, this paragraph must tantalize the employer to want to meet you. No easy task, these few sentences require a strong research base. Project yourself as very valuable, as an original.

The last paragraph should close the sale. Use it to suggest an interview. Offer to present your portfolio. Be sure to mention that you will be calling to schedule a personal meeting in a few days. By promising a call you have already broken ground for future messages. This action closing statement allows you to retain the initiative and exploit the momentum of the process.

A creative cover letter helps amplify your request for the all-important interview. The best cover letters are short but as carefully planned as your resume. Several drafts might be necessary to tune up your personal message. Speak the language of the person reading your letter. Use terminology unique to your profession. Always ask for an interview or indicate that you will call to make an appointment. Keep employers on the hook with your creative cover letter. Play them with the follow-up phone call. Finally, land your target position with a successful interview.

7476 Pecos Drive
Tulsa, Oklahoma 74136
Telephone 918.763.5544

Mr. Tor Arnheim
Principal
HOK Architects/Planners
70 Gateway Drive
St. Louis, Missouri 63052

Dear Mr. Arnheim:

Your presentation at the October AIA/West Conclave involving the Sun River Utah new town concept was very stimulating. Slides of preliminary mass models and schematics indicate a bold new direction in community planning. Friday's Wall Street Journal article announcing project funding through the Getty Foundation prompted me to write you.

I would like to join the HOK Sun River design team. My experience with the DMJM, SOM, and MLTW offices on new town projects uniquely qualifies me for this challenge. The enclosed resume documents publication of my work in Progressive Architecture, Forum, and Domus. My innovative work with solar collection systems should be of particular interest to HOK in this venture.

I'll be passing through St. Louis January 24 to inspect a mall retrofit project in Chicago. Perhaps we could meet either that Monday or on my return trip Thursday, January 27 to discuss Sun River project staffing. I'll call your office in a couple of days to confirm a meeting date.

Sincerely,

Otto Fenwick

Enc: Resume

7021 Drywood Way
Chico, California 95928
Telephone 539.893.6024

Mr. Adam Wells
Art Director
KLA Television
Los Angeles, California 90030

Dear Mr. Wells:

Your assistant, Lori Clark, asked me to send a resume addressed to your attention. Professor Gregg Berryman of California State University, Chico, my advisor and your former colleague indicated that the KLA design group has an immediate opening for a recent university graduate.

While at CSU/Chico, I have pursued a video graphics program with courses in kinegraphics, computer graphics and video editing. Summer internships at KCRA in Sacramento and KPIX in San Francisco have enhanced my professional preparation. I design with Media 100, Video Toaster, Pinnacle and SGI software. My experience also includes non-linear editing to network standards.

I am familiar with the high quality work of your KLA graphics group through recent CLIO tapes. Examples of your program titles were shown in class as significant trendsetters in television graphics. My professional goal has long been to work in the Los Angeles market, for a creative video group with the powerful reputation of KLA.

Thank you for your initial interest. I will telephone your office Tuesday, May 2 to arrange a convenient time for you to review my digital portfolio.

Sincerely,

Kaylee Wilson

Kaylee Wilson

Enc: Resume

114 Seawall Road
Sausalito, California 94555
Telephone 415.722.6024

Mr. Craig Wilson
Design Director
Marketing Plus
Ten Mile High Place
Denver, Colorado 80221

Dear Mr. Wilson:

Three food packaging systems by your firm shown in the July Communication Arts Annual intrigue me. Frankly the level of work is well above the other entries published. For years I have admired the unique Marketing Plus visual approach to consumer packaging, particularly your attention to opening systems.

Wendy Blake of your firm indicated at the last Aspen Design Conference that Marketing Plus plans to open a San Francisco office in late November. My enclosed resume clearly outlines the unique educational and professional experiences I can offer your organization.

My comprehensive knowledge of the West Coast target markets can help Marketing Plus gain an early advantage in this highly competitive region. Extraordinary contacts with suppliers, buyers, and the design community enable me to assemble a world class staff and organization for your new San Francisco office. Trust me to provide the leadership to make Marketing Plus/San Francisco an early profit center.

I will be in Denver on Thursday, September 6 and Friday, September 7 while attending the Packaging Expo. Perhaps we can meet briefly late Thursday afternoon to review my portfolio and package samples. I'll call to confirm your availability.

I look forward to meeting with you.

Very truly yours,

Wes Buckman

Wes Buckman

Enc: Resume

# Resume Etiquette

Your creative resume is a tool, nothing more. If you don't use it, don't expect it to work for you. Even the best-designed resume is useless if it is not applied to self-marketing. Techniques for adapting your creative resume to the job search involve resume etiquette.

The creative resume must help you get an interview or support you during an interview. Consider your resume to be a means rather than an end. Focus your attention on arranging interviews, since this is where the job search is won or lost. Schedule interviews either by letter or telephone. Combine both techniques for maximum impact. Careful research will dictate the accepted scheduling approach in your target market.

Larger corporations, steeped in tradition, may have different interview-scheduling policies from smaller, dynamic firms. Advertising agencies with national clients might expect more formality than small consulting firms. Organizations in the Northeast observe etiquette different from those in the more relaxed Sun Belt. Target your interview search to reach a specific individual in an organization. Avoid personnel departments if possible. They tend to deflect your effort.

Time of year is critical when scheduling interviews. July and August are often difficult, since these are the favorite vacation months of decision makers. June probably has the greatest influx of university graduates entering the job market. The Christmas holidays are uncertain, owing to vacations and travel. Annual report season and tax season can be so hectic internally that many firms find little time for interviewing. Time your interview campaign to coincide with peak hiring periods. The fourth quarter, September through November is best for finding creative positions, followed closely by the first quarter of the year.

The most direct interview method is to arrange an appointment by telephone. Very convenient, phoning can put you directly in touch with the person who will interview you. An initial conversation can help warm things up for your interview. On the other hand, your telephone call may not be able to penetrate the protective layer of people that sometimes insulate creative managers. To beat these executive telephone guards try calling before 8 A.M., during lunch, after 5 P.M., or on Saturday morning. Decision makers often come to the office early, work through lunch, after hours, and even on weekends. Try to reach these busy executives when they are apt to be answering their own phones. Conversations during off hours are less likely to interrupt important office business.

If your phone call hits target, keep your conversation short and direct. Be positive and complimentary. Encourage the interviewer to set a specific interview time. If the firm is extremely busy, suggest a time at the end of the normal working day. Usually the pace slows, telephones stop ringing, and you will receive more time and attention. Try to avoid Mondays, the most hectic day of the week for many interviewers.

| | |
|---|---|
| **ABC/CHANNEL 7**<br>4151 PROSPECT AVE LA CA 90027 | (213) 557-5127 |
| **ABC TELEVISION NETWORK**<br>2020 AVENUE OF THE STARS #200 LA CA 90067 | (213) 557-7077 |
| **CBS/TELEVISION CITY**<br>7800 BEVERLY BLVD LA CA 90036 | (213) 852-2345 |
| **KCOP/CHANNEL 13**<br>915 N. LA BREA AVE LA CA 90038 | (213) 851-1000 |
| **KHJ/CHANNEL 9**<br>5515 MELROSE AVE LA CA 90038 | (213) 462-2133 |
| **KNBC/CHANNEL 4**<br>3000 W. ALAMEDA AVE BURBANK, CA 91523 | (818) 840-4444 |
| **KNXT/CHANNEL 2**<br>6121 SUNSET BLVD HOLLYWOOD, CA 90028 | (213) 460-3000 |
| **NBC TELEVISION NETWORK**<br>3000 W ALAMEDA AVE BURBANK, CA 91523 | (818) 840-4444 |
| **KTLA/CHANNEL 5**<br>5800 SUNSET BLVD HOLLYWOOD, CA 90028 | (213) 460-5500 |
| **KTTV/CHANNEL 11**<br>5746 SUNSET BLVD HOLLYWOOD, CA 90028 | (213) 462-7111 |

You may be asked to mail or fax your resume before an interview has been confirmed. Employers use the resume in this manner to screen your creative qualifications, saving precious interview time for the really serious job seekers. Design your creative resume to power through the screen and set the stage for a face-to-face meeting.

Faxed resumes involve some risk as output quality varies widely. If color or high resolution photography drives the central concept of your resume it's best to avoid fax. The same holds true when an employer requests faxed samples of your work. Why show your portfolio at less than perfect form? Use mail or messenger. Another alternative is to put your resume on an appropriate website.

A second method for scheduling an interview is to mail a resume accompanied by a cover letter. This technique affords you sufficient time to compose a strategic letter, tailored to each employer. Addressed to a specific person in the firm, the letter will usually reach that person without interference. Never address this package with the company name alone. Never mail your resume without a cover letter. Aim your resume directly at the creative manager to improve your chances of an interview.

Another way to set up an interview is to coordinate mailing with a telephone call. For this technique to work well you need to predict delivery accurately. If the postal schedule is uncertain, use a registered letter or courier service to guarantee delivery and attract the attention of an employer. Simply mail your resume with cover letter and call the day of delivery or the day after to request an interview. An impression of your resume is fresh in the mind of an employer during the telephone conversation. This technique allows you to demonstrate organization and planning skills while at the same time showing an employer the importance you attach to personal contact.

Whether arranging interviews by telephone or mail, avoid asking if any jobs are available, positions are open, or hiring is taking place. Creative positions tend to be filled in unusual style. Rather than ask for a job, ask for a review of your portfolio. Most creative supervisors and art directors empathize with your eagerness, having experienced it themselves. They enjoy interviewing during slack work periods; in fact, part of their job is to discover new talent. If you take this approach, the least you will get is valuable feedback. In addition, you are apt to receive employment leads and reference approval. Do not worry about a job offer. It will come naturally if you and your creative resume make a good impression.

# Interview Research

Before beginning your interview campaign ask yourself "Where do I want to live?" Plan your first job in one of the 50 or so major media markets. If you do not prefer an urban lifestyle, commute to the city while living outside. Only the major markets have concentrations of large clients, good budgets, and top creative personnel. In the larger markets you can change jobs without changing cities.

After you settle on a city, move there while you schedule interviews. A permanent base will allow you to take the pulse of a market and investigate it thoroughly. Plan for 10 to 20 interviews. It will take that many to expose you and your work to the market. Word travels fast on the creative grapevine, once you make it known that you're available. Even if you receive a job offer after your first or second interview, follow your game plan. Other offers may be much better. By interviewing all of your targets you can build your reputation in the market. Contacts you make during the interview process inevitably help in your next job search.

Develop a strategy to help decide where you want to work. Large corporations pay well, offer fine benefits, and require more teamwork. Some creative people find corporate employment stifling, while others thrive on structure and a "single-client" in-house responsibility.

Advertising agencies offer great earning potential and a quick pulse. Job changes may be frequent as major clients come and go. Design studios function as consultants to solve visual problems for many different clients. Graphic designers need to be productive, flexible, and available to meet tight deadlines.

Book publishing, with its rich tradition, offers a satisfying career, although salaries can be lower. Publication design including periodicals, annual reports, and marketing collateral is attractive if your interests are editorial. Exhibit design, environmental graphics, and package design require a three-dimensional sensitivity. The large budgets involved may lead to great financial reward. Multimedia design, information design, web design, game design, and e-commerce offer dynamic careers in the virtual world. Match what you most want to do with those firms doing it best to select your interview targets.

Research plays a major role in your self-directed job search. Creative positions are seldom listed in newspaper classified sections. Most openings are filled through word of mouth and personal referral in the creative underground. A handful of highly specialized placement agencies and headhunters focus on experienced personnel. Use national and regional placement websites to sample your market and narrow your choices. Timing and luck also play a major role. Account changes, new clients, contract awards, and business cycle changes all contribute to job availability.

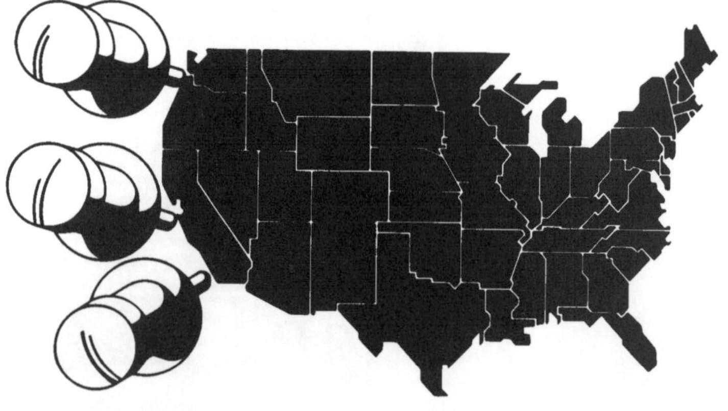

Start your research online. Websites provide very fertile research data on most employers. In short order you can review project profiles, personnel biographies, and studio philosophies. Some sites even include application and portfolio review policies.

In addition telephone yellow pages, directories, journals, periodicals, and awards annuals may be helpful. Contact art directors' clubs, advertising organizations, and public relations societies for references. After you locate the name, title, and telephone number of a target individual, use an index card or personal organizer to catalog each prospect. As your interviews progress, note pertinent names, dates, times, telephone numbers, and comments. Regularly consult and update your file. Keeping your interview information organized is well worth the time investment. This focusing process helps you to build a valuable resource for future reference.

Build your target file before you start to interview rather than during the process. Prioritize your list by shuffling your reference cards in the order of target preference. Interview only after you collect significant data on each firm. Research the size of an organization, number of offices, and important clients. Learn the age of a company, its competitors, and how it has grown. Get a copy of its corporate annual report. Determine its reputation and how employees are treated. See if the visual output of your target firm is published in creative periodicals and annuals.

Some standard reference sources can be particularly helpful. Most are available in university or metropolitan libraries. Moody Manuals, Dun and Bradstreet Million Dollar Directory, Standard and Poor's Register of Corporations, and The College Placement Manual detail the corporate sector. Information on government agencies appears in the Federal Career Directory and the United States Government Manual.

Detailed data on creative firms is available in The Creative Black Book, the Literary Market Place, the Standard Directory of Advertising Agencies, Standard Rate and Data Service, and The Design Index. Use the Art Index and Reader's Guide to Periodical Literature to locate significant articles in *Print, Communication Arts, International Design, Step-by-Step, HOW, Wired, Graphis, Novum, Metropolis, Advertising Age*, and *Ad Week*.

Careful research of target firms and their representatives will prepare you to interview intelligently. You will not have to ask redundant questions during the interview. You will demonstrate that you are truly prepared and have more than just a casual interest in the organization. More important, being informed will boost your confidence and help you make a strong impression.

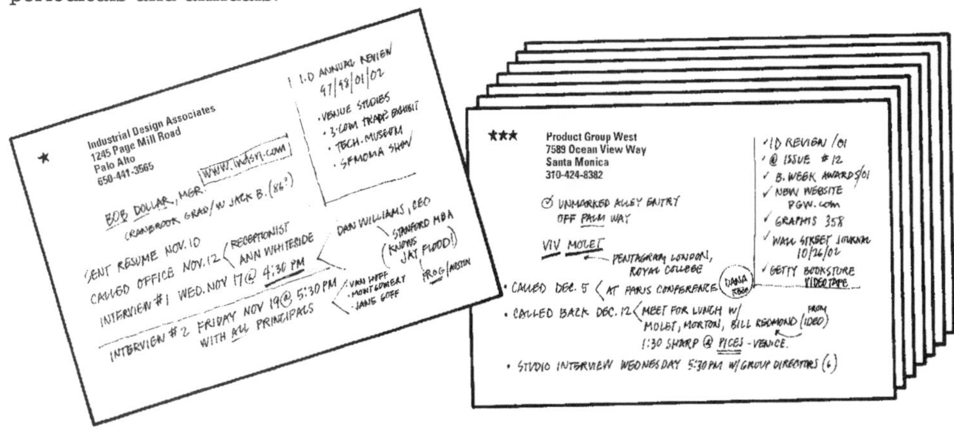

# Creative Interview

Your creative interview is the big event. Dress for it. Select your clothing for a job level higher than the one you seek. Although interviewers in creative professions may dress less formally than their corporate or banking counterparts, you should aim for a stylish conservative appearance. Your suit or outfit should be dressy and businesslike. Dark colors make the best initial impression. Appear clean, neat, and well-groomed. Keep jewelry, perfume, and aftershave scents subtle. Never smoke or chew gum. Look professional, articulate, and ready to start work at the time of the interview.

Be on time for your interview; better yet, arrive 15 minutes early. Plan a couple of hours between appointments for recovery time and transportation contingencies. Your interview may last longer than planned, particularly if the employer is really interested. While waiting you might chat with the secretary or receptionist. Start to make your positive impression at the front desk. The secretary can help you get in for an interview, and make you feel comfortable while waiting. You might even become co-workers in the future.

Store several resumes in your portfolio. Keep them in a clearly marked envelope separate from other work samples. Besides protection, careful storage will help you to avoid a panic search. Extra copies will come in handy if more than one interviewer is present. You may be asked for additional resumes to be passed on to decision makers not attending.

As you begin the interview, present your resume. It will serve as an effective icebreaker. Let the interviewer lead and pace the conversation. Plan to expand on your resume data. Be sure to present your resume before showing a portfolio. Expect the employer to glance at your resume throughout the review process. Your creative resume helps to guide the flow of your interview.

Radiate an enthusiastic self-confidence. Smile and maintain eye contact throughout the interview. Express your alertness with positive body language. Try to appear relaxed while maintaining an upright posture.

Avoid interrupting the interviewer, a most annoying habit. Cutting short a sentence or stopping the conversation before a point is completely made will certainly offend the interviewer. Yet don't hesitate to ask questions. This is a chance to draw upon your preliminary research. You can ask about key design personnel. Request information on significant projects in process. Inquire about corporate growth. Most experienced interviewers are flattered by good questions if you phrase them properly. Praise the work quality of the firm if you truly respect it.

At an opportune time in the interview emphasize precisely how you might help the company. Articulate your unique qualifications. Envision a connection between yourself and the firm. Explore how you might fit the organization and add to it. Avoid asking directly for a job, but try to sell yourself so convincingly that the interviewer will feel obligated to discuss hiring.

If you present a portfolio during the interview, prepare to answer questions about your work. The portfolio reveals your ideas, hand skills, and problem-solving ability. Plan to defend your visual decisions. Expect to justify your creative concepts. Briefly describe the problem and the rationale for your solution. Never make excuses for your portfolio work; it must succeed at face value and speak for itself.

One way to anticipate and prepare for interviewing is to role-play with a critical friend, your professor, or college placement personnel. Rehearse for the creative interview to ease your anxieties. Many colleges offer video facilities that enable you to view practice interviews and improve your performance. Your professors probably have professional contacts who will help you with a dress rehearsal. Take advantage of practice opportunities to help you through the first two or three appointments. After those you will certainly feel more comfortable.

Questions likely to arise include the self-assessment type that interviewers use to test you. What can you do for us? What results have you produced? Why would you want to work here? Why should we hire you? These frequently asked clichés can be very revealing. Prepare a few short, creative responses. Rehearse them and you'll pass with flying colors.

When you sense the end of the interview is drawing near, ask for some feedback. You may not even have to ask, as criticism is part of the standard language of creative professionals. Some interviewers will be kind, some extremely harsh, with the others in between. During the interview accept any criticism gracefully. Avoid arguments at all cost, even if you vehemently disagree. Remember that criticism is only the opinion of one person. Feedback from an interview, when taken as advice, can only improve your next opportunity. Use the interview critique to help modify your portfolio, refine your target research, and streamline your verbal responses.

Do all you can to close the interview on a positive note. Certainly a warm thank you and firm handshake are in order before leaving. Successful closure involves more than just a cordial parting. Find out where you stand. In a subtle manner suggest that you would like to phone back to keep in touch. Ask if the interviewer would recommend a colleague or another firm that might be interested in your work. Many fine positions are located with these special leads. Indicate your availability for a future interview. Leave a lasting impression with your interest, sincerity, and persuasiveness. Follow the interview with a brief thank-you note or letter to complete the creative interview cycle.

If you make a good impression, your timing is fortunate, and a position is open, an offer may come your way. Be patient! Your interview process at large agencies or corporations can involve several interviews with individuals, corporate officers, and management committees. Small firms might feel comfortable with repeat meetings to verify initial impressions. Strive to make a strong impact in successive meetings, revealing additional positive traits.

Consider these useful negotiating techniques when discussing salary. Telephone professional societies for the salary ranges of the position in your target market. Wait until the employer makes an offer. If you are asked to name your salary requirements, politely decline. You can be sure that any open position has already been budgeted. Indicate that you are considering other offers. Employers as a rule offer higher salary figures than prospective employees themselves quote. If it proves impossible to avoid the big question, mention a high figure, a strong starting point for negotiation. If a salary range is mentioned, begin negotiations at the top of the scale to improve your strategic bargaining posture.

Some positions include benefits and perks. Examine carefully offers of automobile, insurance, stock options, or profit sharing. Healthy benefit packages might help compensate for low starting salaries. Beware of accepting any job offer during an initial interview. Postpone your acceptance for a few days. Take the time to compare other offers. A reasonable gestation period may influence the employer to raise the initial offer for fear of losing you. A few days or a week to consider an offer is within reason. Wait too long and you'll lose your negotiating leverage and the opportunity.

Salary is only one component of employment. At least as important is your opportunity to work with top creative talent in a stimulating environment. Consider the challenge of the position. Examine your chance for personal growth. Weigh your work responsibilities. Remember that most creative people make frequent job changes early in their careers. Moves are made for additional exposure, responsibility, and compensation. Initially seek a challenge, and financial reward will follow.

If you are fortunate enough to find a position where your daily activities don't seem like work, then your job search will have paid rich dividends. Individuals able to give to a position more than they take from it are lucky indeed. The stimulation and satisfaction of creative work contributes immensely to your life, to the lives of your family and co-workers, and to society. If your creative resume helps you get the interview that leads to rewarding employment, then this book will have achieved its goal.

# Creative Resumes

More than 80 creative resumes are reproduced in the remainder of this book. Examine them closely. Each resume began as a dream and a blank sheet of paper. Each reflects the development of a unique idea. Some of the resumes evolved quickly, while others were born of considerable sweat and rework. Notice how every creative sample conveys a dominant "Big-Idea." Each reflects some unique trait of its designer. All of the resumes shown reach beyond the expected to stimulate an interview.

Sample resumes are grouped in order of experience. Those shown first were created to land an internship, co-op position, or summer job. Next appear resumes that were developed concurrently with visual portfolios to seek entry-level positions. Creative resumes by experienced professionals complete the selection.

Production requirements for this book necessitated showing most resumes at 85% of original size, some smaller. By viewing all the resume samples in black only, you can focus on form and content.

Examples are included for your creative stimulaltion. Learn from the resume samples but do not copy them. Imitation contradicts the very concept of this process. Push your own resume well beyond the samples shown. Remember, yours will be unique only if it mirrors your special attributes. Use the examples as visual springboards to help you design your ideal creative resume.

# Brian  Steele

542 Nord Ave. #12
Chico, CA 95926
916-893-0836

**Work experience**
El Rey Theatre, Chico CA Duties- Doorman, candy cashier, usher. In charge of of promotional graphics.
May 1992/Present

Mangia, Tiburon CA Duties- Table support service. May 1991/September 1991

Chinese Kitchen, Corte Madera CA Duties- Cashier, Delivery Person. October 1989/August 1990

**Relevant courses**
Type One
Graphic Viz
Computer Graphics
History of Graphic Design
Ad Copywriting
Script Writing

**Mac Literacy**
Aldus Freehand
Super Paint
Mac Draw
Mac Paint
Adobe Photoshop
Mac Word

**Awards/Competition**
Earth Day 1992 Poster/T-shirt

Butte County Health Dept, Second Hand smoke competition

**Activities**
Member of Designers in Progress
Basketball, fishing, and tennis

PERSONAL
Laura
Carpenter
899
Warner
Street
Chico
California
95926
916
345
6258

EXPERIENCE
Impulse Spring, 1980
CSUC Yearbook 1979-80
1980-81
Art Director
Design Workshop Fall, 1981 and Spring, 1982
University Relations October, 1980 to January, 1982
Receptionist
Handsel's 1979
Gift Wrapper

EDUCATION
Publication Design
Typography
Copy Preparation
Graphic Arts Principles
Photography
Corporate Identity
Package Design
Environmental Graphics

MEMBERSHIPS/AWARDS/SEMINARS
ADAC 1981-present
Designers in Progress 1981-present
Honor Award: Poster 1982 Student Design Show
California State Scholarship Award 1976
Envision 4, 5
Business of Design Fall, 1981

References
available
upon
request

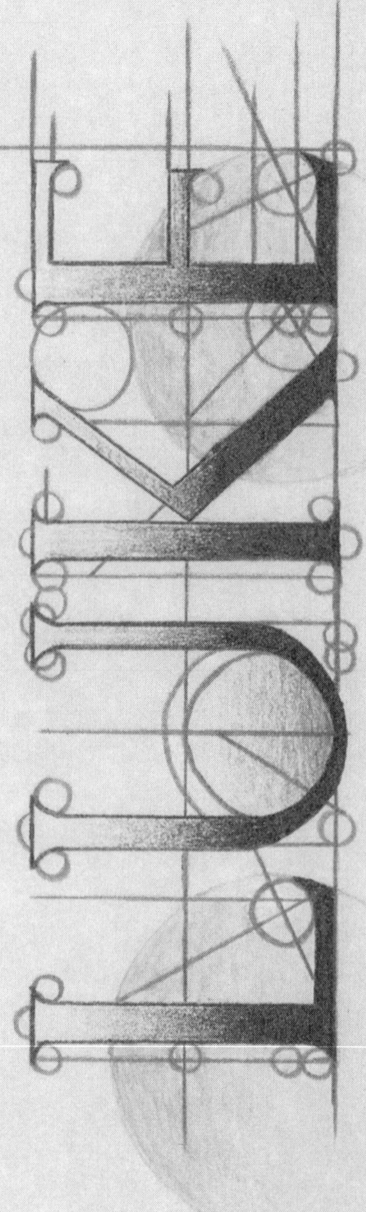

*luke wilson*

926 Alder Street Chico, Calif. 95928
phone:530-893-3913 other:530-520-4706

*accomplishments*

designed 1997 Earth Day (poster & t-shirts)

designed 1997 Endangered Species
Fair t-shirt for the Butte Environmental Council

designed logo for Fontaine Construction Co.

passed portfolio review

*education*

graduated 1994:Mira Costa High School
Manhattan Beach, Caliifornia

Currently attending California State University, Chico
major: communication
emphasis: graphic design

applicable courses: drawing, painting,
color theory, history of graphic design,
letterforms, photograhy, typography,
graphic visualization, electronic print/publishing

*work experience*

Round Table Pizza Hermosa Beach, Ca.
1.5 years: 1992-94 counter person, cook

Mike Mack's Water Ski School
Parker, Arizona 1 summer: 1995
ski instructor, retail proshop, salesperson

Ron Wilson Construction Inc. Lawndale, Ca.
6 summers: 1991-97 misc. construction
and property management: framing, concrete,
painting, finish work, minor plumbing and
electrical

Mary Ordorica
Graphic Designer
4130 Nighthawk Way
Chico, CA 95973
345-5280
email ordorica@aol.com

*Fables are foundations of common sense, shots at uncommon sense, and human tradition that is formed from universal experiences. Graphic Design ideas are also formed from these concepts, usually with an added twist.*

**A thirsty crow**
**found a pitcher with**
**some water in it,**
**but so little was there that**
**try as she might,**
**she could not**
**reach it with her beak,**
**and it seemed as though**
**she would die of thirst**
**within sight of the remedy.**
**At last she hit upon a clever plan**
**She began dropping pebbles**
**into the pitcher,**
**and with each pebble**
**the water rose a little higher**
**until at last it reached the brim,**
**and the knowing bird**
**was enabled to quench her thirst.**

**Necessity is the mother of invention**

**AEsop's Fables**

## Experience

Currently doing volunteer work, teaching art at Notre Dame School.

Participated in fundraising and design ideas for the Fall Festival, Spring Gala Auction, graduation, and yearbook at Notre Dame School.

## Memberships

School Board member for Notre Dame School 1994-1995.

Member of the Long-range Planning Committee for Notre Dame School 1994-1995.

Girl Scouts of America Troop leader 1992-1997.

Member of the Butte-Glenn Medical Society Alliance 1985-1997.

## Education

Bachelor of Arts Degree in Graphic Design 1999, Minor Fine Art
*California State University, Chico*
Studied Ad design, Typography, Illustration, Letterforms, and Computer Graphics. Skill in Adobe Illustrator, Adobe Photoshop, and Adobe Pagemaker. Able to work on Macintosh and IBM platforms.

Fine Arts major 1983-1985
*California State University, Sacramento.*
Studied Etching, Lithography, Color design, Sculpture, Ceramics, and Art History.

Associate in Arts Magna Cum Laude graduated 1977 from *Nassau Community College,* Garden City, New York.

The year was 1989 and **Kari Caldwell** was in the eighth grade when she got her first **taste** of graphic design and realized it was her destiny. Since then, she has been passionate about all forms of design, especially typography. Her first real experience in print was at Durham High School where she was editor of the yearbook. Although her design skills had a simple **flavor** at the time, she was thrilled to see her work in print and **hungry** to further her knowledge of design. After graduating eleventh in her high school class, Kari made the move to Butte College where she quickly enrolled in as many design classes as possible. It was there that she gained **fresh** new insight and **sweetened** her love of design. Upon receiving her AA and after much deliberation, Kari made the crucial decision to remain in Northern California and attend Chico State, where she is currently enrolled. Her class load has included Graphic Visualization, Typography, History of Graphic Design, Computer Graphics, Color Theory, Photography and many Drawing classes. As a result of these courses, her skills are **new and improved!** Kari has also supported herself for the past two and one half years through a part time job at Raley's Supermarket. From a designer's perspective, she has realized that the benefit of working at a grocery store is that it allows for plenty of time to study and critique packaging design. She has successfully learned to combine the responsibilities of work and school, just like a **well balanced meal**. And if that were not enough to keep her busy, she also coaches the Chico All Star Dance Team and led them to a first place finish at a national competition in March of 1998. Kari plans to graduate from Chico State in the Spring of 1999, but not before **satisfying her appetite** for much more design knowledge.

**1114 Nord Ave. #8 • Chico, Ca. 95926 • (530) 898-2696**

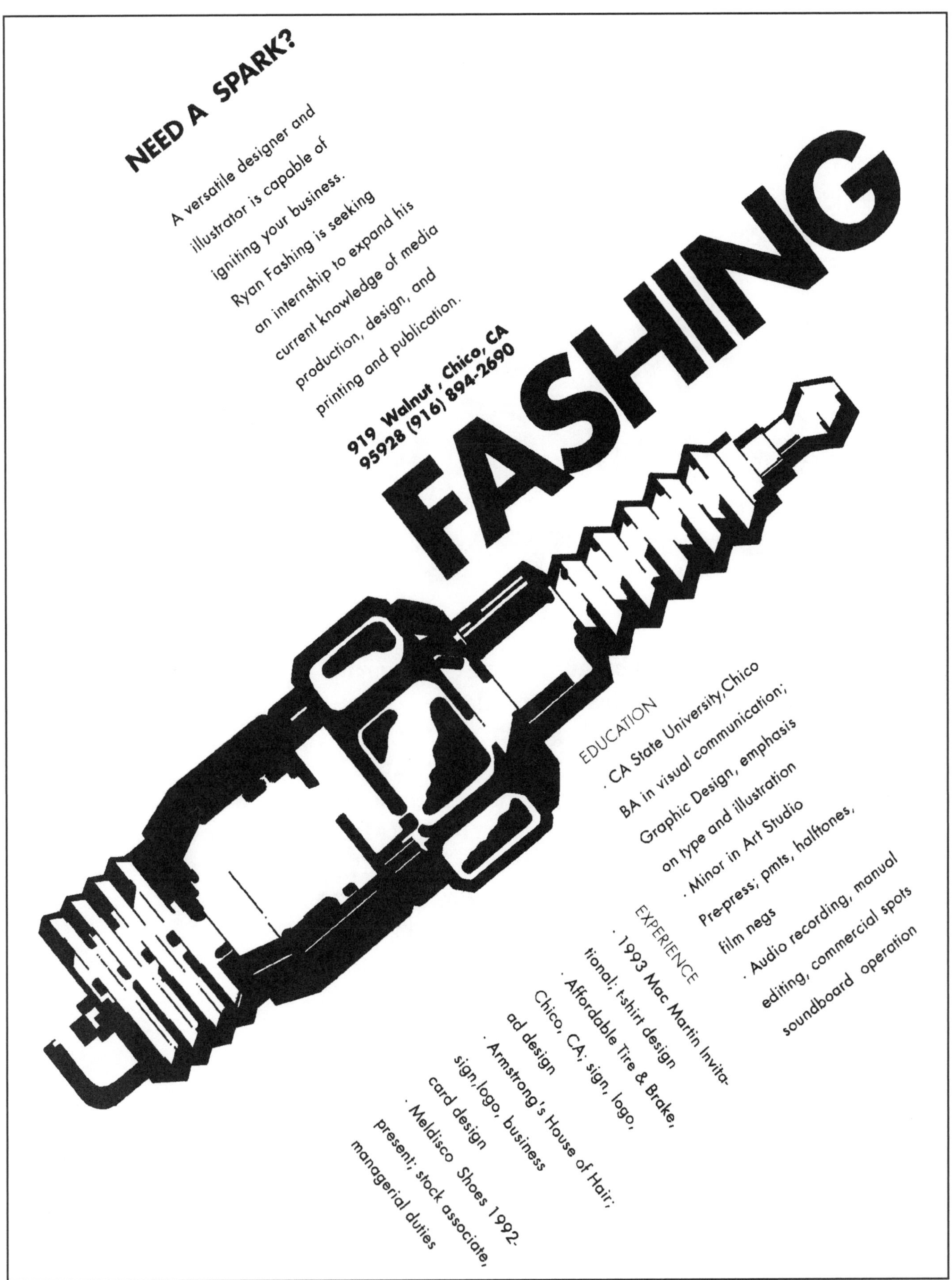
NEED A SPARK?
A versatile designer and
illustrator is capable of
igniting your business.
Ryan Fashing is seeking
an internship to expand his
current knowledge of media
production, design, and
printing and publication.
919 Walnut , Chico, CA
95928 (916) 894-2690
FASHING
EDUCATION
. CA State University,Chico
BA in visual communication;
Graphic Design, emphasis
on type and illustration
. Minor in Art Studio
Pre-press; pmts, halftones,
film negs
. Audio recording, manual
editing, commercial spots
soundboard operation
EXPERIENCE
. 1993 Mac Martin Invita-
tional; t-shirt design
. Affordable Tire & Brake,
Chico, CA; sign, logo,
ad design
. Armstrong's House of Hair;
sign,logo, business
card design
. Meldisco Shoes 1992-
present; stock associate,
managerial duties

# Jay Chiat
# Ross Van Dusen
# Karen Curry
# Lee Clow

Not yet, but because I have a passion for Chiat/Day, maybe this summer!

I'm a team player; count on me to enthusiastically interact with your creative groups and deliver assignments on time. My experience as a team member both at Macy's and as a clothing buyer for Santa Rosa Community College Bookstore was a pleasure.

Depend on me to both write and visualize. At C.S.U. Chico, I'm a Communications major with a focus on Graphic Design. My experience includes copywriting, marker rendering, typography, reprographics and photography. Three semesters on the Dean's List is a measure of my dedication. I'm eager to benefit from your dynamic agency.

I'll telephone in a day or two to schedule an interview for a Chiat/Day summer internship.

***Paul Brown***

1824 Ashmeade Court San Jose, CA 95125 ☎ 408.371.2948 ***Education:*** California State University Chico, Bachelor of Arts in Visual Communications, 1990. West Valley College, Associate of Science in Park Management,1985. ***Experience:*** 1986-1990; free-lance design. Clients include U.S.Bureau of Land Management, Chico Heritage Association and Cook Family Rice Inc. 1988-1990; graphic design CSUC Instructional Media Center. Responsibilities include: Concept development, client consultation, camera ready art using Macintosh computers with page maker and freehand software, stat camera operation. 1987-1990; photogragher for CSUC Art History Department. Used copystand to shoot slides for Art History instruction. ***Awards:*** 1990 CSUC annual student design show: honor awards in logo, poster, t-shirt and illustration design. 1989 CSUC student show: Best of show awards in illustration and package design, honor in logo design. 1988 CSUC student show: best of show in technical illustration and landscape photography, honor in package design and illustration. ***Memberships:*** Art Directors and Artists Club of Sacramento. Designers in Progress, CSU, Chico. ***Interests:*** fishing, windsurfing, photography, back-packing. ***Immediate career goals:*** I am seeking a professional environment in which I can further refine my design and illustration communication skills.

Justin Page
229 west 6th st Chico, Ca 95928
530•893•0547
jpage@ecst.csuchico.edu

*Student designer/illustrator seeks design work to explore, refine, and contribute skills. Can help bring life to any Project.*

## applications

**Editorial Designer.** *The Orion.* (Paid Intern) Responsible for design and layout of a section of this national award winning student run newspaper. Contributed illustrations and typography to layouts. **Ad designer.** *The Orion.* (Paid Intern) Worked with sales representatives to design ads for contracts ranging from 45$ to 460$. Learned the pressures and responsibilities of meeting and making deadlines. Worked in **retail, food service, construction**, and **automotive** environments over the last seven years. Traveled alone to the middle of Alaska to work at Denali National Park.

## studies

Currently studying **Graphic Design**,
California State University Chico.
Chico, CA
**G.E.**, College Of Marin.
Kentfield, CA. *1993-1996*
**G.E.**, Contra Costa Community College.
Richmond, CA. *1996*
El Cerrito High School.
El Cerrito, CA. *Graduated 1993*

## awards

**Deans List Student,** CSUC. *1997*
**Honor Roll Student,** College of Marin. *1995-1996*
**Honor in photo journalism,** Juried student show, CSUC. *1997*

mustang@ecst.cuchico.edu
408.255.2727
1560 Bonnie Joy Avenue
San Jose, California 95129
**Greg Storey**

On March 2, 1974, a small pink wrinkled boy took his first breaths in his newly illuminated world. Under the watchful eye of his parents, the young Greg Storey grew.

His thirst for knowledge guided him through four years at Lynbrook High School in San Jose, California. Before he graduated in 1992, he completed an ROP Commercial Art program at Monta Vista High School in Cupertino. His desire to be a Graphic Designer led him to enroll at CSU Chico, the first stepping stone towards realizing his dream.

After three enlightened years at Chico State, Greg received many academic honors. He made the Dean's List for all six semesters and became a member of the Phi Eta Sigma, Phi Kappa Phi, and Golden Key honor societies. He became active in Designers In Progress, a student organization that brought designers such as David Goines, Josh Stallings, Glenn Matsui, and Steve Stone to Chico to offer insight and wisdom.

Greg was the winner of a T-shirt design contest for scholastic achievement among Chico State football players. He won an award in the annual juried show among Chico State students for his Yo-Yo postcard. He won national recognition in a costume design contest for Mike Allred's Madman Comics.

As Greg continued to grow, so did the technology around him. In response, he learned the Macintosh and programs such as Illustrator, Pagemaker, QuarkXPress, Photoshop, Streamline, Authorware and, Director to prepare for both print and the electronic media.

It became apparent that not all knowledge could be found in the classroom. Subsequently, as Storeytime Productions, Greg attracted freelance design creating T-shirt, vehicle, and waterbottle images for Chico State student organizations. During the summer, he worked at the Disney Store in San Jose to help strengthen his interpersonal communication skills.

He also began working during the school year at the Presentation Graphics Lab, a self-service computer center designed to help students and faculty create and output high-end electronic files.

For Greg, life is a journey not a destination. Although what lies ahead may at times be rough, he will always meet life head on with the same desire and tenacity that has propelled him all along.

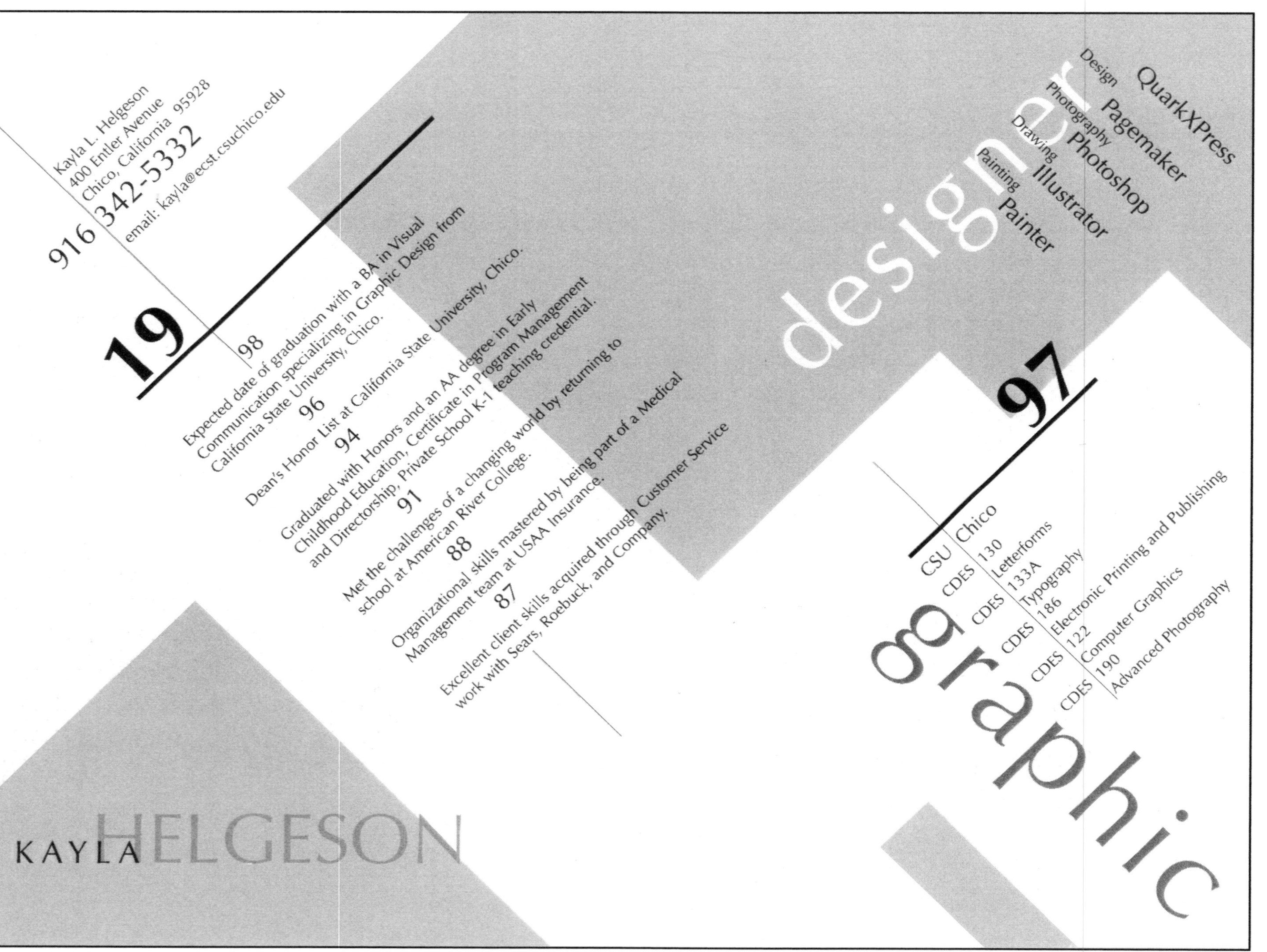

KAYLA HELGESON
graphic
designer
QuarkXPress
Design Pagemaker
Photography Photoshop
Drawing Illustrator
Painting Painter
97
CSU Chico
CDES 130 Letterforms
CDES 133A Typography
CDES 186 Electronic Printing and Publishing
CDES 122 Computer Graphics
CDES 190 Advanced Photography
19
98 Expected date of graduation with a BA in Visual Communication specializing in Graphic Design from California State University, Chico.
96 Dean's Honor List at California State University, Chico.
94 Graduated with Honors and an AA degree in Early Childhood Education, Certificate in Program Management and Directorship, Private School K-1 teaching credential.
91 Met the challenges of a changing world by returning to school at American River College.
88 Organizational skills mastered by being part of a Medical Management team at USAA Insurance.
87 Excellent client skills acquired through Customer Service work with Sears, Roebuck, and Company.
Kayla L. Helgeson
400 Entler Avenue
Chico, California 95928
916 342-5332
email: kayla@ecst.csuchico.edu

# kimberly bickel

p.o. box 1037...chester...california...96020...916.258.4248

## education

1992 bachelor of arts degree *visual communications*...csu, chico
with emphasis in...publication design...corporate identity...typographic design
package design...calligraphy...photography...advertising copywriting

## experience

1991–1992 *graphic designer*...instructional media center...csu, chico
responsibilities included...development of concepts for publications, brochures, posters, flyers, programs, and signs
consultation with clients...computer production in pagemaker, freehand, and quarkxpress...camera-ready art
computer generated mechanicals to negative output...direct consultation and contact with printers
1989–1992 *waitress*...r.fish and co....chico
1981–1988 *waitress*...knotbumper...chester

## honors & membership

1992 commencement...csu, chico...*outstanding visual communications student*
1992 student show...csu, chico...*honors for publication design*
1991 student show...csu, chico...*honors for photography*
1990–92 *designers in progress*...csu, chico

## conferences

1992 *42nd international design conference*...aspen
1992 *envision 18*...sacramento
1991 *envision 17*...sacramento

*references available upon request*

# GOOD FOR ONE EXPERIENCED DESIGNER

**Features—** Outgoing, enthusiastic and creative designer educated to fill design position with professional firm. Formulated with specific interests in publication design, editorial design, conceptual design, web design, project coordination, client interaction, copywriting and production.

**Highlights—** Prepared with high quality skills in graphic design, computer graphics, typography, letterforms, web design, photography and color theory. Positioned on the Dean's List every semester. Highly skilled in the Macintosh OS and design applications including QuarkXPress, Illustrator, Photoshop, and web software.

**Professional Specs—** Work experience includes editorial, advertising, and web design for *The Orion*, CSU, Chico's award winning broadsheet newspaper. High quality digital imagesetting and color proofing at Grade-A Graphics, Santa Cruz, CA. Mac OS computer technician for CSU, Chico's Media Preparation Lab. Other work interests include soccer officiating and landscape maintenance.

Designer is president/founder of the Chico State Wildcat Water Polo Club, was vice-president of Phi Eta Sigma honors society, and is currently a member of communication clubs: Designers in Progress and Graphic Arts Technology Organization.

**Extras—** Personal interests include gourmet cooking, photography, mountain biking, and snowboarding. Favorite typefaces include: Futura and Garamond.

**Interested individuals please contact Beau Smith for interview or for references at 530-894-1193.**

# KIMBERLY CLARK

GRAPHIC DESIGN

PO Box 9155
Santa Rosa, CA 95405
707.576.1456

## EDUCATION

Bachelor of Arts Degree in Visual Communications. California State University, Chico. 1988. Emphasis: Package Design, Corporate Identity, Lettering, Graphic Visualization, Computer Art, Typography, Reprographics, and Photography.

Santa Rosa Junior College. 1985. Doyle Scholarship recipient. Emphasis: Photography and Drafting.

R.O.P. Graphics program at Montgomery High School, Santa Rosa, California, 1982.

## EXPERIENCE

Internship. Landor Associates, International Headquarters: San Francisco. Summer 1988. Graphic design and production for Brand Identity and Corporate Identity.

Scott Architectural Graphics, Santa Rosa. 1983 to 1986. Photographer, darkroom technician, graphic production, installations, shipping and receiving.

Shutterbug Camera Shops, Santa Rosa. 1979 to present. Graphic design and production, interior/exterior store signage, data entry for inventory control, darkroom technician in minilab, retail sales clerk.

Clark Graphic Design

## ACTIVITIES

Designers In Progress 1986 to 1988

John J. Sorbie poster workshop 10.88

ADAC San Francisco Design Tour 04.88

World Travel: Italy, Hong Kong, China, Mexico

References available upon request

- Darren Knowles
- Honest
- Talented
- Out Going
- Responsible
- Kind
- Artist
- Dynamic
- Casual
- Funny
- Alert
- Friendly

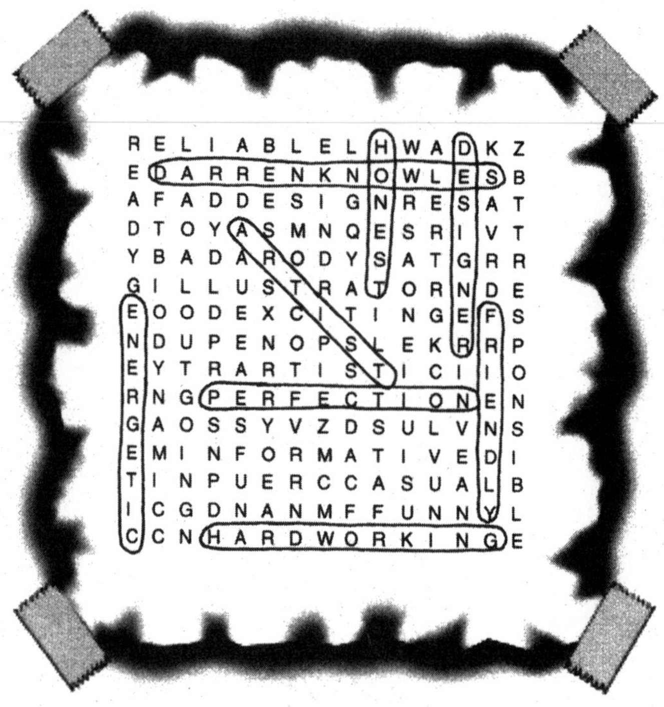


- Exciting
- Reliable
- Designer
- Artistic
- Ad Design
- Energetic
- Fun
- Informative
- Perfection
- Hard Working
- Illustrator
- Ready

**Darren Knowles**
15025 Humbug Road
Magalia, California 95954
(530) 873-3159

## Personal Information

Currently attending California State University Chico, pursuing a Bachelor of Arts degree in graphic design.

Enjoys the outdoors. Free time consists of camping, fishing, hiking, and swimming.

Everyday hobbies include, basketball, softball, golf, scuba diving, and playing pool.

## Awards and Honors

Voted most creative by the students and faculty of Paradise High School, senior year, 1991.

Painted a mural for the Paradise High School administration in 1989 of the school's Mascot.

## Work Experience

*Albertsons Grocery Store*
Journeyman Clerk/ Produce
6636 Clark Road
Paradise, California 95969
September 1993 to Present.

*All The Best Video*
Customer Service Clerk
14586 Skyway
Magalia, California 95954
February 1992 to November 1994.

*Marriott Desert Springs*
Valet Parking Attendant
Palm Desert California
August 1991 to February 1992.

## References

Jeff Hodsdon
6458 Berkshire Way
Paradise, California 95969
(530) 877-8233
Friend/ Manager, Five years

Brandon Giraldez
9642 Columbine Court
Magalia, California 95954
(530) 873-4135
Friend/ Co-worker. Ten years

Bryan Taylor
5462 Dean Way Road
Paradise, California 95969
(530) 876-4090
Friend, 15 Years

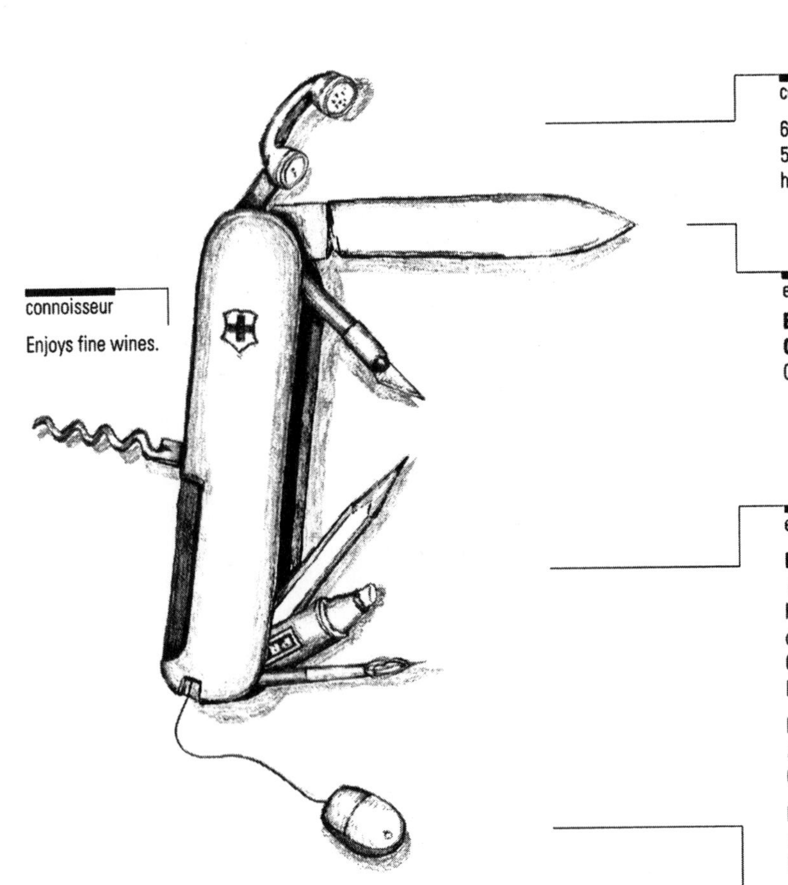

contact

621 Pomona Avenue #38, Chico, CA 95928
530.898.3211 • mumford@shocking.com
http://www.shocking.com/~mumford

education

**BA** in Communication Design
**Certificate** in Electronic Printing and Publishing
California State University, Chico *May 1998*

experience

**Design Internship,** Presentation Graphics Lab,
*1997 - 1998*
Production work. Troubleshooting with Macs. Operate output devices such as Poster Maker, Vinyl Cutters, Screen to Slide, CD burning (Toast), Fuji Photo Printer, Cannon Cyclone with SGI Interface, slide and leaf scanning.

**Design Internship,** Steve Wong & Associates,
*Summer 1997*
Computer production design and digital prepress work.

**Design Internship,** Arts and Humanities Dpt., CSU, Chico,
*1996 - 1998*
Designed and produced posters promoting various campus events.

**Park Aide/ Design,** Pfeiffer Big Sur State Park,
*Summer 1996*
Designed all park information signs. Conducted campfire programs once a week with crowds of over 200.

**Design Internship,** The Orion campus newspaper,
*1995 - 1996*
Worked with sales reps to design and produce advertisements for nationally acclaimed school newspaper. Designed and produced the Classified section.

**Disc Jockey**, KCSC 95.5 fm,
*1994 - 1996*
Conducted a weekly radio show with music format for the community of Chico.

computer skills

| | | |
|---|---|---|
| Photoshop 4 | QuarkXpress 4 | Pagemaker 6.5 |
| Freehand 8 | Illustrator 7 | Director 6 |
| HTML 3.2 | BBEdit 4 | Painter 5 |
| Streamline 3 | Microsoft Office 97 | Superpaint 2 |
| Quicken 7 | Suitcase 3 | MacOS8 |

awards/achievements/associations

**Designers in Progress (DIP),** *1996-1998*
**Student Show Award,** CSU, Chico Design Department, *1997*
**People to People Student Ambassador,** Australia, *1993*

# Robert I. Mumford

**DRYOPITHECUS**
*3 million*

**Objective**

As a creative graphic designer and illustrator, I not only follow in the footsteps of a long line of visual communicators, but I strive to lead the way with innovative ideas to present information.

**A. ROBUSTUS**
*2 million*

**Employment**

Freelance design
Chester 1980-1987
Wide variety of design and illustration including graphics for courtroom procedure, mural, logos, charts, t-shirts, brochures, etc.

Seneca District Hospital
Chester 1976-1980
Medical records transcriber,
medical staff librarian, medical staff secretary, in charge of skilled nursing facility records, admitting clerk, discharge clerk.

**H. ERECTUS**
*500,000*

**Education**

Bachelor of Arts
Visual Communication
CSU, Chico 1985
Emphasis on illustration, corporate identity, environmental graphics, packaging, kinegraphics, lettering, copywriting, publication design, typography, airbrush.

Associate of Arts
Business Administration
with Art minor.
Cabrillo Community College

**H. SAPIENS**
*300,000*

**Internship / Membership**

Graphic Design Internship
Instructional Media Center
CSU, Chico 1985
Concept development, client consultation, preparation of camera ready art, use of compugraphic headliner and stat camera.

Member of Plumas County Arts Commission, Almanor Arts Association.

**A. GRIFFITH**
*Modern*

**Personal**

Alicia Carole Griffith
P.O. Box 994331
Redding, CA 96099
916•243•0604
Married with two grown daughters. Interests include cross-country skiing, hiking, and painting watercolors.

References available upon request.

# DESIGNER FOR HIRE

***Face**—Belongs to **Craig Hedges**. Twenty-three years old, healthy and hard working.*

***Ideas**—Large supply. Tend to run rampant upon release.*

***Old business card** still in pocket—Image Group, Inc. (Chico, CA). 4/79-3/81. Conceptual design, project coordination, client consultation, copywriting and production. Also Stoner Advertising. (Enid, OK). 2/78-12/78. Conceptual design and production primarily for print advertising.*

***Shirt sleeves**—works in them frequently.*

***Class ring**—From California State University, Chico, Class of 1980. BA in Visual Communication. Studied advertising design, corporate identity, publications, typography, photography, copywriting, information and communication studies. Also attended Phillips University (Enid, OK). Studied Advertising design, drawing, painting, art history, and had one semester of foreign study.*

***No wedding ring**—Just a few close calls.*

***Portfolio**—Short but sweet. Why not take a few minutes to look at it? Craig will be calling for an appointment in a few days or you can call him at (213) 287-7488.*

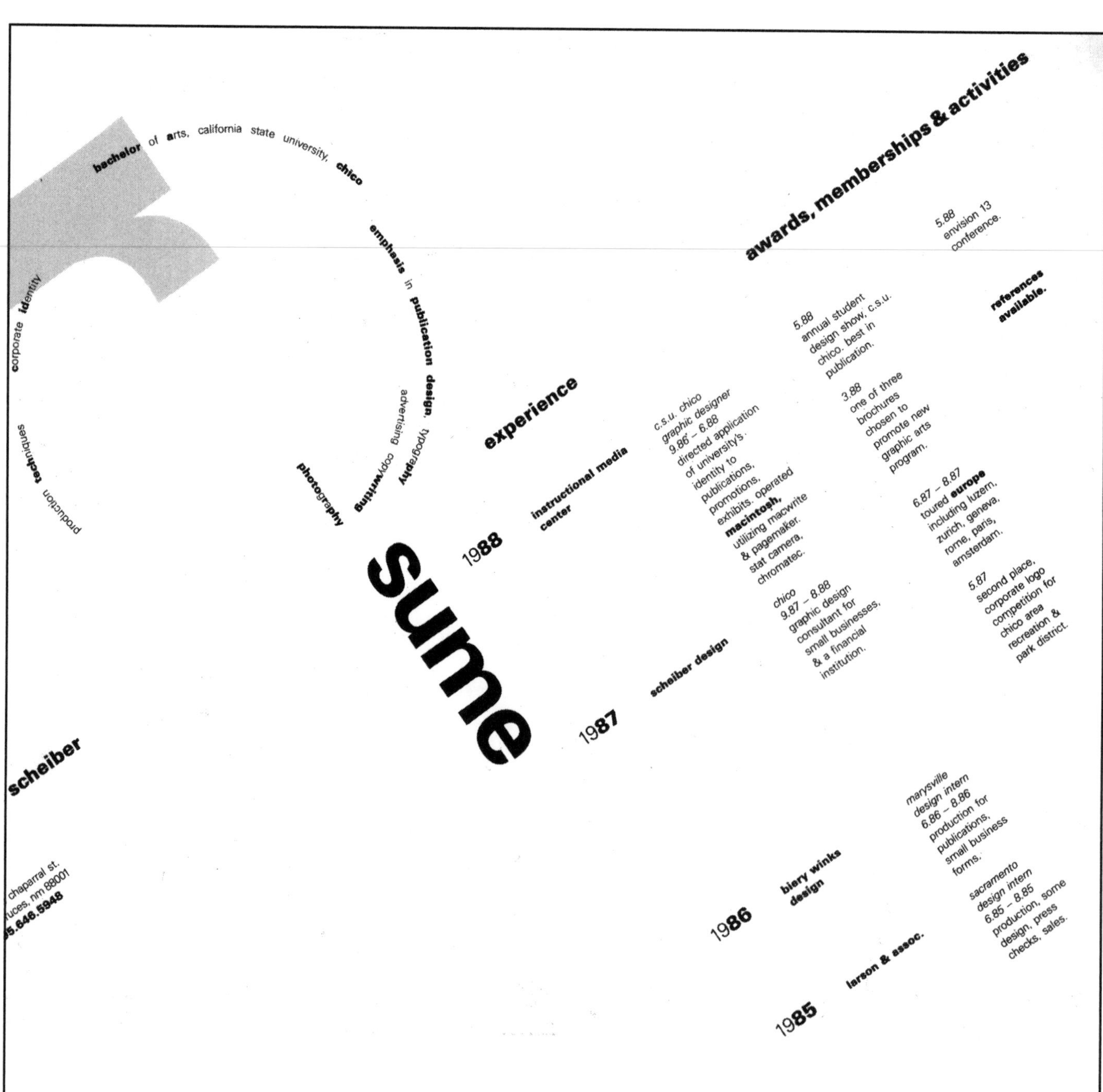
bachelor of arts, california state university, chico
emphasis in publication design, typography
advertising copywriting
photography
corporate identity
production techniques
scheiber
chaparral st.
luces, nm 88001
5.646.5948
sume
experience
1988
instructional media center
c.s.u. chico
graphic designer
9.86 – 6.88
directed application of university's identity to publications, promotions, exhibits. operated macintosh, utilizing macwrite & pagemaker. stat camera, chromatec.
1987
scheiber design
chico
9.87 – 8.88
graphic design consultant for small businesses, & a financial institution.
1986
biery winks design
marysville
design intern
6.86 – 8.86
production for publications, small business forms.
1985
larson & assoc.
sacramento
design intern
6.85 – 8.85
production, some design, press checks, sales.
awards, memberships & activities
5.88
envision 13 conference.
5.88
annual student design show, c.s.u. chico. best in publication.
3.88
one of three brochures chosen to promote new graphic arts program.
6.87 – 8.87
toured europe including luzern, zurich, geneva, rome, paris, amsterdam.
5.87
second place, corporate logo competition for chico area recreation & park district.
references available.

Education:

BA Graphic Design,

**CSU, Chico.**

December, 1993.

Coursework:

Publication Design,

Typography,

3-D Animation,

Marker Rendering,

Graphic Pre-press,

Photography,

Illustration,

Other Coursework:

Communication Criticism,

Communication Research,

Communication Theory,

Scriptwriting,

Ad Copywriting.

Work Experience:
**Chico News and Review**:
Ad Design and
Illustration Intern,
fall 1993.
**West Coast Lettering
and Athletic Inc**:
design and camera ready
art for silkscreen,
spring 1991.
**Gallo Design**:
Graphics and mechanical
art for clothing.
Clients included:
CSUC Residence Halls,
Chico State
Volleyball tournaments,
Gupwear Sportswear
and Beach-It Sportswear.
**Potter Signs**:
design and production of
exterior signs,
1987-88.

Clubs and memberships:
Designers in Progress,
fall 1993.
CSUC Men's Volleyball Clut
1990-93. President, 1992.

1520 La Linda Ln.
Chico, CA 95926
**916.895.0185**

# Mark Gallo

Computer design skills:

Aldus Freehand,

Aldus Pagemaker,

Quark Xpress,

References available
upon request.

# susan leeson

*1290 Melton Drive, №2*

*Yuba City, CA 95991*

*916.751.9223*

## EDUCATION

*B.A. Degree in Graphic Design,*
*California State University Chico, Fall 1995*
*A.A. Degree, American River Jr. College, Spring 1992*

*Relevant courses: Communication theory courses, typography, reprographics, ad design, letterforms, graphic visualization, computer assisted art, photography, color theory, drawing and painting, ad copywriting, and history of graphic design.*

## COMPUTER EXPERIENCE

*Macintosh: Painter 2.0, Adobe Illustrator, Aldus Pagemaker, Adobe Photoshop and QuarkXPress*

## WORK EXPERIENCE

*Freelance*
*Business icon, illustrations, logos, and mural*

*Body Express*
*Fitness Instructor 1992 – present*
*Membership Director 1992 – 1995*

*United Spirit Association*
*N.B.A. Sacramento Kings Fastbreak Dancer 1990 – 1992*
*Dance/Drill camp instructor 1989 – 1991*

## HONORS AND AWARDS

*Invitation to the Golden Key National Honor Society*
*Dean's Honor List, Chico State: 1993, Spring 1994 and Fall 1994*
*Highest Honors, American River Jr. College*
*2nd place, Sacramento Savings Bank Art Competition 1994*
*Merit Award, Sacramento Savings Bank Art Competition 1993*
*Fred G. Wade Scholarship, Advertising Club of Sacramento 1992*
*Citizen's Scholarship Foundation of America 1992, 1993, and 1994*
*Art Purchase Award, San Juan High School 1989*
*1st place, Congressional Art Competition 1988*

## MEMBERSHIPS

*National Honor Society of Phi Kappa Phi*
*Designers in Progress, Chico State*

## REFERENCES

*Gregg Berryman*
*Graphic Design Professor, Chico State*
*916.898.6872 wk 916.343.6500 hm*

*Chris Ficken*
*Art Director, Instructional Media Center*
*916.898.4421*

*Bobbi Long*
*Graphic Design Professor, Chico State*
*415.663.9303*

E d u c a t i o n

CWC
Denver, Co.
Dean's List
1960-61

Univ. of Colorado
Boulder, Co.
1961-63

CSU
Chico, Ca.
Communication
Design
1992-94

Studying

- Drawing
- Color Theory
- Photography
- Graphic Vis.
- Copy Writing
- Typography

Corporate
Reprographics
History
Packaging
Publication
• *completed*

Ann White Brown
242 Tom Polk Circle
Chico, Ca.
916 343-8677

Computer Skills — Mac Pagemaker — PC Windows

Goals — Short Term Internship — Long Term Art Director

# White Brown

E m p l o y m e n t

## Texas

Democratic Party
1976-88
Special Events
and
Print Coordinator

R e f e r e n c e s

Bob Slagle
Chairman,
Texas Democratic
Party

Dwayne Holman
Political
Consultant
Austin, Tx.

Gregg Berryman
Design
Professor
CSU, Chico

# MARCIE WILSON

345 W.Sixth Street
Chico, CA 95928
(916) 894-5593
*local*

–or–

3445 Klamath Woods Place
Concord, CA 94518
(510) 676-7055
*permanent*

## EDUCATION

**1989 - present** California State University, Chico. Will receive a Bachelor of Arts Degree in Visual Communications in May 1994. Courses in Typography, Environmental Design, Corporate Design Systems, Packaging, Reprographics, Art History, History of Graphic Design, Visual Communication Concepts, Color Theory, Photography, Computer-Assisted Art, and Scriptwriting. Good skills with airbrush.

## EXPERIENCE

**1992** Graphic Design Internship for one full year at the Regional Center for Continuing Education. Computer-aided design as well as traditional paste-up.

## COMPUTERS

Extensive fluency of Pagemaker, Freehand.
Good skills with Illustrator and Microsoft Word.
Very computer-literate, willing to learn Quark Xpress and other programs.

## ACTIVITIES

Member of Designers in Progress since 1990
Attended Envision Student Poster Workshop and Envision 17 Conference
Attended lecture given by Wolfgang Weingart in San Jose (Oct.1991)
Received Bank of America Achievement in Art award 1989

## PERSONAL

Born in New York 1971. Lived in Saudi Arabia for seven years, and the most recent twelve years in California. Interested in traveling and foreign cultures, traveled to Europe in 1989 visiting various museums and observing differences in visual communications.

## REFERENCES

**Tricia Whitworth**
Center for Regional and Continuing Education, California State Univ., Chico

**Gregg Berryman**
Professor: Visual Communications, California State Univ., Chico

# **Peter** Fine

# **Graphic** Design

**P.O. Box 11423**
**Glendale, AZ 85318-1423**
**602.937-3298**

## At School

Bachelor of Arts degree
**Visual Communications**
California State University, Chico, December 1993
Studies included publication design, typography, corporate identity, packaging, marker rendering, letterforms, reprographics, copywriting, media writing, and communication theory, research and criticism.
GPA 3.5

Associates in Arts degree with Honors,
June 1990,
American River College, Sacramento, CA.

## On the Job

Instructional Media Center,
California State University, Chico
Chico, CA
January 1992-June 1994
**Graphic Designer**
Responsibilities included consultation with clients and printers, the design development and production of publications, brochures, posters, programs, slides, and signage. Most of these projects were produced on the Macintosh and printed directly to film. Managed the graphic design studio, summer 1993.

Sacramento News & Review
summer 1991
**Illustration Intern**
Assigned illustrations to accompany editorial and advertising for a weekly metropolitan paper.

Instructional Media,
American River College, Sacramento, CA
September 1990-June 1991
**Student Assistant**
Worked with graphic designers to produce brochures, teaching aids, posters, and signage. Most projects were produced on the Macintosh.

Western Contract Furnishers,
Rancho Cordova, CA
May 1989-February 1990
**Advertising Assistant**
Assisted creative director with corporate identity system, marketing, advertising and mechanicals. Other projects: furniture showroom displays, model home installations, trade shows, photos and signage.

## Mac Mastery

Adept with: **Illustrator & Quark**
Familiar with: Freehand, Pagemaker, Photoshop and Persuasion

**Teaching Assistant**
Adobe Illustrator,
American River College, spring semester 1990

## Clubs & Kudos

**Awards**
Outstanding Graphic Design Student 1993/1994, CSU,Chico
Graphic Design Program Scholarship, 1992
CSU, Chico
Honors Illustration, Annual Student Show, 1992
CSU, Chico.

**Member of**
The Honor Society Phi Kappa Phi
DIPS—Designers in Progress, CSU, Chico
AIGA

## References

Available at your request.

JULIE COX

THANK YOU

I appreciated the opportunity to visit your studio, and to show my portfolio. Your time, as well as your input, was very helpful.

JULIE COX

PERSONAL

5340 Rae Lane
Redding, CA 96003
916 549 3940

REFERENCES

Gregg Berryman, Professor of Graphic Design; C.S.U. Chico, California.
Office 916 895 6872/Home 916 343 6500

Joe Martin, Art Director of A.S. Marketing Studio; C.S.U. Chico, California.
Office 916 895 6411/Studio 916 895 4624

Robert Beckrest, Director of Robert Beckrest Design and Advertising; Stockton, California.
Studio 209 473 3223/Home 209 334 5245

# JULIE COX

**PERSONAL**

5340 Rae Lane
Redding, CA 96003
916 549 3940

**EDUCATION**

1987 California State University, Chico; Received a Bachelor of Art in Communication Design and a Minor in Art Studio.

1982-1984 University of California, Davis; Majored in Fine Art and Biological Science.

**EMPHASIS**

Corporate Design, Environmental Design, Publication Design, Package Design, Graphic Visualization, Lettering, Typography, Ad Copywriting, Script Writing, Airbrush and Illustration.

**EXPERIENCE**

1986 Associated Students, Marketing Studio; C.S.U. Chico; Graphic Design Intern. Projects included designing visual identities, advertisements, point of purchase displays and collateral.

1986 Robert Beckrest Design and Advertising; Graphic Design Intern. Responsible for thumbnails, mechanicals and brochures. Operated vertical stat camera.

1986 St. Joseph's Hospital of Stockton; Graphic Design Intern. Prepared community relations materials, posters and brochures.

**AWARDS**

Graduated Magna Cum Laude from the College of Communication, C.S.U. Chico. Dean's Honor List for three semesters.

Received Best of Show in Logo Design and Environmental Design categories at the 1987 Juried Student Show.

References on request.

Dean Kojima
229 West 6th Street
Chico, CA 95928
530-893-0547

EXPERIENCE

February 2000–May 2000

ASHTON ABECK DESIGN
*Designer*
Creating concepts for corporate identity, business systems, business collateral, worked on a team to design websites, and acquired bids from printers.

September 1998–December 1999

CALIFORNIA STATE UNIVERSITY, CHICO
*Student Designer*
Worked at the Instructional Media Center in the *Print Graphics* department as an intern for 1.5 years. Saw each project from initiation to completion. Responsibilities included client meetings, project management, design, budgeting, and prepress.

September 1997–December 1997

*THE ORION* NEWSPAPER
*Ad Designer*
Collaborated with several ad representatives to create or reproduce advertisements for local businesses.

EDUCATION

California State University, Chico 1999 BA in Communication Design, Emphasis Graphic Design

DESIGNER'S IN PROGRESS
*President*
While president of this graphic design club at CSU, Chico, I was able to bring in speakers like Doyald Young and Craig Frazier, organize workshops, and provide opportunities to experience the top graphic design firms and printers in Sacramento and San Francisco. We also participated in community events and retained a membership of 75 students.

EUROPE
Backpacked for three months through 10 different countries expanding my ideas on design, expanding my mind with culture, and filling my life with adventure.

REFERENCES

Allen Ashton
*Principal*, Ashton Abeck Design

Gregg Berryman
*Professor*, CSU, Chico

Alan Rellaford
*Professor*, CSU, Chico

** References & portfolio available upon request.*

# MERI JUNE

Merijune Tokuno
5715 W. Elverta Rd
Sacramento, CA 95837
916.925.0019

*Education*
1985-1988
California State University, Chico
BA, Visual Communications

1982-1984
University of California, Davis
Psychology

1980-1982
American River College
Sacramento, CA
AA, General Education

*Experience*
Summer 1987
Internship
Advertising Designer
Chico News & Review
Responsibilities:
Production included
preparation of camera ready art
and type specification

Summer 1986
Cashier/Counter Person
Flash 1 Hour Photo
Sacramento, CA
Responsibilities:
Processed film
provided customer service
and quality control

Fall 1984
Manpower Temporary Service:
Roche Biomedical Laboratory
Sacramento, CA
Responsibilities:
Stamped, photocopied, filed and
mailed medical forms

*Related Classes*
Publication Design
Typography
Environmental Graphics
Corporate Identity
Reprographics
Photography
Copywriting
Lettering
Script Writing
Graphic Visualization

*Computer Literacy*
Apple Macintosh
Software usage:
MacDraw, MacWrite
Microsoft Word
SuperPaint and PageMaker

*Memberships*
1985-1988
Asian Christian Fellowship
California State University, Chico
Executive Committee Member
Activities Coordinator
Monthly Program Designer
1983-1985
Davis Christian Support Group
University of California, Davis
1982-1983
Asian Student Union
University of California, Davis

*References/Portfolio Available*

# TOKŪNO

# Sara Waters

5 Hardwood Court
Pleasant Hill, CA 94523
415 825-1293

**EDUCATION**

**1990**
**California State University, Chico**
**Bachelor of Arts in Visual Communication, Minor in Painting**

**Related courses: publication design, corporate identity, advanced typography, reprographics, communication theory, research and criticism, advertising copywriting, creative problem solving and photography.**

**EXPERIENCE**

**1990**
**CSU, Chico, Graphic Design Intern. Designed posters for the College of Humanities and Fine Arts. Worked with clients from initial consultation to final approval of camera-ready artwork. Included extensive use of the Macintosh IICX with emphasis on Freehand 2.0 and Pagemaker 4.0.**

**1986-1991**
**Art Etc., Chico, Picture Framer. Designed and produced custom framing, wrote and signed company checks, prepared deposits and ordered supplies.**

**AWARDS/HONORS**

**1990**
**CSU, Chico Student Design Show**
**Best in Poster Design**
**Best in Publication Design**

**1990**
**Contra Costa Club**
**Identity Competition**
**Third Award**

**1987-1990**
**Dean's Honor List, CSU, Chico**

**1988**
**CSU, Chico Student Design Show**
**Honor Award in Photography**

**MEMBERSHIPS**

**1990-1991**
**Art Directors and Artists Club**
**Sacramento, California**

**1989-1990**
**Designers in Progress**
**Student organization, CSU, Chico**

**1987-1988**
**Chico Symphony Orchestra**
**Second Oboe**

**References available upon request**

**Education**

*1997*

California State University, Chico

Bachelor of Arts Communication Design

Minor in Studio Art

**Work Experience**

*1994–1997*

Presentation Graphics Lab

Chico, CA

Responsibility included scanning flatbed images and slides, printing digital images via Canon laser color, black and white, poster and Fuji photo emulsion printers, creating vinyl lettering, and customer service problem solving.

*Summer 1996*

Powell and Associates

Newnan, GA

Member of team which designed corporate identities and collateral.

**Macintosh**

Proficient in QuarkXPress, Photoshop, and Illustrator. Working knowledge of Freehand, Pagemaker, Director, Authorware, and Web development.

**Greg Storey**

1560 Bonnie Joy Avenue
San Jose, CA 95129
408.255.2727

**Awards and Honors**

Member of Phi Kappa Phi Honor Society
Member of Phi Eta Sigma Honor Society
Member of Golden Key Honor Society
Member of Dean's List for nine semesters
1997 Outstanding Graphic Design Student
1997 Graduated cum laude
1997 Winner of Chico Airshow poster design contest
1996 Recipient of Graphic Design Program Scholarship
1995 National Winner of *Madman Comics* costume design contest

**Extra Curricular Activities**

*1993–1997*

Member, Designer in Progress

Held positions of Treasurer, Vice-President, and President.

*1994–present*

Storeytime Productions

Freelance design for water bottles, wearables, CD's, posters, illustrations, postcards and Web graphics.

**References available upon request**

graphic designer

kelsie park-sherbo
267 Fairview Road
Ojai, CA 93023

Good design is an influential part of a successful business. Whether you're in the business of promoting yourself, or promoting a service, a well designed resume, ad or brochure is critical in making that lasting impression. I am a Senior at Chico State University majoring in Communication Design. I'll be graduating in a year and am home for the summer looking for anyone interested in design work being done for them or their business. I can do anything from business cards to web pages. I have advanced skills on the Macintosh and have experienced dealing with service bureaus. My rates are reasonable and my work is of high quality. I am a motivated and enthusiastic person that loves what I have chosen to do in my future. Let's meet for coffee sometime to discuss your design needs!

805.646.7950 ! kelsieps@ecst.csuchico.edu ! http://www.ecst.csuchico.edu/~kelsieps

ANN BRITTON

503. 645.7667.

## EDUCATION

1995, BACHELOR OF ARTS
VISUAL COMMUNICATION DEGREE
CALIFORNIA STATE UNIVERSITY, CHICO
EMPHASIS IN TYPOGRAPHY, PUBLICATIONS, PACKAGING, MULTI–MEDIA, CORPORATE IDENTITY, LETTERFORMS, MARKER RENDERING, REPROGRAPHICS, COPYWRITING, COMMUNICATION THEORY, COMMUNICATION RESEARCH, AND CRITICISM

20715 NW CHILOQUIN CT
PORTLAND, OREGON 97229

## ON THE JOB

1994–1995, GRAPHIC DESIGN, IMC GRAPHICS
INSTRUCTIONAL MEDIA CENTER, CSU, CHICO
RESPONSIBILITIES INCLUDED CONSULTING WITH CLIENTS AND PRINTERS, DEVELOPING THE DESIGN AND PRODUCTION OF PUBLICATIONS, BROCHURES, POSTERS, PROGRAMS, LOGOS, SLIDES, AND SIGNAGE. ALL PROJECTS WERE PRODUCED ON THE MACINTOSH AND MOST WERE PRINTED DIRECTLY TO FILM

1994–1995, BRITTON DESIGN
FREE LANCED FOR A LOCAL CHIROPRACTIC BUSINESS, DEVELOPED MARK AND APPLIED BUSINESS SYSTEM
LOCAL MARSHAL ARTS STUDIO, APPLIED BUSINESS SYSTEM
LOCAL PRINT SHOP, DESIGN AND PRODUCTION OF BROCHURES, POST CARDS, BUSINESS CARDS, AND INVITATIONS

1991–1993, GRAPHIC DESIGN ASSISTANT, AMY HAMPEL DESIGN, RESPONSIBILITIES INCLUDED CONSULTING WITH CLIENTS, PHOTOGRAPHERS, AND PRINTERS
DESIGN AND PRODUCTION IN FREEHAND AND PAGEMAKER, CAMERA-READY ART, TRADITIONAL AND DIGITAL MECHANICALS

## MAC SKILLS

PROFICIENT IN
QUARKXPRESS,
FREEHAND,
PHOTOSHOP
COMFORTABLE WITH
MACROMIND DIRECTOR,
PAGEMAKER
EXPERIENCED WITH
LEAFSCAN AND
FLATBED SCANNERS

## ACTIVITY

1991–1995
DESIGNERS IN PROGRESS (DIPS), CSU, CHICO

## HONOR

1995, BEST IN PACKAGING, ANNUAL STUDENT SHOW

## REFERENCES

AVAILABLE UPON YOUR REQUEST

## anthony scott albright

### learning

1993, bachelor of arts degree VISUAL COMMUNICATIONS, csu, chico

related classes: typography, publication, environmental, advertising, senior design workshop, corporate identification, packaging, and copywriting

### stuff i've done

1991–1993, GRAPHIC DESIGNER, IMC graphics (instructional media center), csu, chico

responsibilities included ☛ developing ideas for signs, programs, flyers, posters, brochures, and publications ☛ consultation with clients ☛ computer production in QuarkXPress, FreeHand, and PageMaker ☛ camera-ready art ☛ traditional mechanicals and straight to negative computer mechanicals ☛ direct consultation and contact with printers and clients

1992, PROJECT for environmental graphics ☛ chosen for permanent application in bidwell museum

1991, PROJECT for design workshop ☛ received first place for game concept and design

### clubs and things

designers in progress (DIPS), csu, chico

AIGA

### circuitry and gismos

| | |
|---|---|
| QuarkXPress 3.1 | Macintosh |
| FreeHand 3.1 | Microtec scanner |
| Photoshop 2.5 | slide scanner |
| PageMaker 4.2 | stat camera |

### where to find me

1260 vineland avenue

st.helena, california 94574

707.963.7502

### what others think

references if asked

Aware that her school days are coming to a close, our heroine promptly sits down to make a list of all her skills. She begins by describing her love affair with graphic design and photography, then proceeds to list her "life experience" jobs like working in a print shop and dealing cards in Reno. As she writes, she fondly remembers her days as a photographer's assistant and her success in passing the portfolio review at Chico State. With each word she gains new confidence. She has been on the Dean's list each semester! While in school she successfully completed design work for clients such as Vitae, Music Now and Rhythm Magic! Confident that she has what it takes to be a world–class graphic designer, our heroine decides that all she needs now is for someone to give her a chance...

Gillian Hersh 760A Vallombrosa Avenue Chico, CA 95926 916.891.8146

Max Williams
66 Shields Ln.
Novato, CA 94947

mfwilliams22@hotmail.com
415.897.7911 or
415.897.8689

**Education**

*California State University Chico,*
Chico, CA
Degree: Bachelor of Arts in Communication Design

*Santa Rosa Junior College,*
Santa Rosa, CA
Degree: Associate of Arts

"Without play, there would be no Picasso. Without play, there is no experimentation. Experimentation is the quest for answers."

—PAUL RAND

**Work Experience**

- *Associated Students Bookstore*
  11/00—08/01
  Chico, CA
  Designer
  Advertisements, brochures, flyers, posters, signage.
- *O'Reilly & Associates*
  Summer 2000
  Sebastopol, CA
  Designer
  Advertisements, brochures, flyers, posters, signage.
- *Olsten Staffing Services*
  Summer 1999 & Summer 1998
  Novato, CA
  Various Jobs
  Mostly warehouse and office work.

"As Designers we are, as a group, measurably responsible for the visual form of our culture."

—SAUL BASS

**Achievements**

DIP (Designers In Progress)

Berryman Family Graphic Design Scholarship Award

Marin Education Foundation Scholarship

Bank of America Achievement Award in the field of Art

"Give me the luxuries of life and I will willingly do without the necessities"

—FRANK LLOYD WRIGHT

**Computer Skills**

QuarkXPress

Photoshop

Illustrator

Freehand

"We are called to be architects of the future, not its victims."

—BUCKMINSTER FULLER

# Jason Bell

2074 45th Avenue
San Francisco, CA 94116

415.665.3421

"Graphic **Design** is not controlled by technology. Technology **is** controlled by design."

## Education

**California State University**, Chico, BA Visual Communication; Graphic Design, May, 1998, 3.6 GPA

**Studies include:**
Typography, Letterforms, Corporate Identity, Brand Identity, Publication Design, Web Design, Advertising Design, Environmental Signage, Color Theory, Photography and Copywriting

## Memberships

**Designers in Progress** (Vice President)
CSU/Chico 1997/98

**Art Directors and Artists' Club**
of Sacramento 1997/98

## Computer Skills

**Proficient in the following programs:**
Quark XPress, Pagemaker, Illustrator, Freehand, Photoshop, Streamline and Macintosh Operating System

## Experience

**Design Studio Internship**
McNally Temple and Associates, Sacramento: Brochure, Logo, and Collateral Design; Collaborated with printers, photographers and copywriters

**Pre-Press**
Presentation Graphics Lab, California State University, Chico: Computer Tech., File preparation, Client Adviser and Graphic Production Artist

**Editorial Design**
The Orion, California State University, Chico Newspaper: Page Layout and System Design

**Sign Design**
California Customs, sign shop, Sacramento: Computer Tech., Sign Design, Production and Installation

**Freelance Clients**
Bi-Tech Software
Pete Balda, Sierra Mortgage Company
California State University, Chico

## Awards

**Print Magazine**
International Senior Student Cover Competition: Fifth Place
Design to be published in the November/December, 1998 issue of Print

**Envision 23**
Design Conference National Student Poster Competition: High Honors

**Student Show**
California State University, Chico: Honor Award for Corporate Identity

**Orion**
California State University, Chico Newspaper: Awarded Best Editorial Designer, while the Orion received a Pacemaker for design, and was awarded Best of Show.

**Academic**
Named to the Dean's Honor List for six consecutive semesters

References are available upon request.

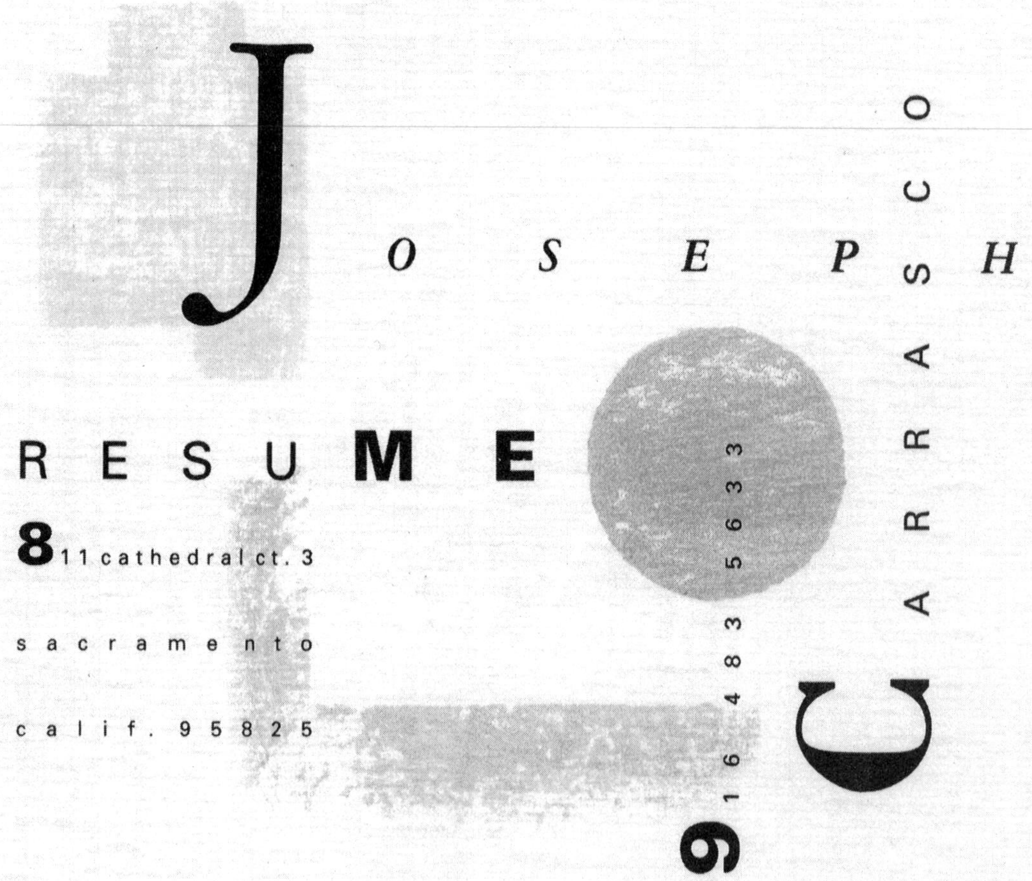


EDUCATION

Bachelors of Arts,
Visual Communications
Minor in Art Studio
California State University, Chico, 1989
*Emphasis in Corporate Identity, Package Design, Typography, Visual Communication concepts and Creative problem solving.*

California State University, Sacramento
1984 - 1987
*Emphasis in Art Studio.*

EXPERIENCE

Graphic Artist
Firefighter Publications
July - December 1990
*Responsibilities include layout and design of newsletters, business systems, flyers and promotional items utilizing Microsoft Word, Pagemaker and Adobe Illustrator applications on the Apple Macintosh computer, paste-up, preparation of camera ready art, and use of ITEK camera processor.*

Shop Representative
Quik Print
June 1989 - June 1990
*Responsibilities included customer service, paste-up, and bindery.*

INTERNSHIP

Graphic Designer
Associated Students Marketing
California State University, Chico
September 1988 - May 1989
*Responsibilities included the design and layout of a poster, a T-shirt and flyers using the Macintosh computer, design and production of environmental displays and signage.*

AWARDS

National Association of Campus Activities Conference
1988 Graphics Competition:
*Second Place - One color poster*

JOSEPH CARRASCO
811 Cathedral Ct. #3
Sacramento, CA 95825
**916 • 483 • 5633**
*references upon request*

# RESUME'

**PERSONAL**

Larry V. Will
681 South Tustin Avenue
Suite 111
Orange, California 92666
(714) 538-0310

**EDUCATION**

Associated Arts Degree
Cerritos College, Norwalk

Bachelor of Fine Arts Degree
Visual Communications Major
California State University, Long Beach

**EXHIBITS/AWARDS**

Young Designers Competition
C. Braun Company
Certificate of Merit

National Paper Box Association
Rigid Box Design Competition
First Place Award

31st Annual Art Directors Club of Los Angeles Show of Advertising and Design In the West 1976 Distinctive Bullet Award

Departmental Scholarship 1976
California State University, Long Beach

Departmental Award 1974
Cerritos College, Norwalk

Cerritos College Annual Student Art Exhibit, 1975
First Place Award

Cerritos College Annual Student Art Exhibit 1974
First Place Award

**EXPERIENCE·**

Gallery Assistant
Cerritos College, Norwalk
Director: Gilbert Steel

As assistant I constructed installations which were used for exhibits. Also helped organize the design of the exhibits which included placement of lighting, color coordination, and displaying of type.

Staff Artist
Cerritos College, Norwalk
Publications Director:
Jay Malinowski

While attending Cerritos I started in the publications department as an assistant to the staff artist. When he left his position, until placement was made, I took over the duties of staff artist. In this position I was involved in most of the campus printed material for community and campus programs. Duties included concept direction for all art work, full production coordination, including camera involvement for reproduction purpose, and press checking for quality control of printing.

Production/Layout Person
Martin Wayne Advertising
3270 Cherry Avenue
Long Beach, California 90807

While attending CSULB I worked part time for Martin Wayne as a production and layout person. Most of the job material I worked on was collateral for clients such as, Long Beach Gas Co., Riccar International, and the Bragg Co. My duties varied according to individual job involvement, from doing complete production to layout and design.

**FREELANCE DESIGN**

During my senior year at CSULB I contacted a company regarding some design work. I ended up totally designing a complete visual communications package. This package included a company identity for stationary, packaging, and signage. Since graduating from CSULB I have continued to keep this company as a client and have used my professional services to fill their visual marketing needs.

**REFERENCES**

George Turnbull
Professor
Center for Information and Communicational Studies
California State University Chico
Chico, California 95929

Jim VanEimeren
Professor
Visual Communications for Design
California State University, Long Beach
(213) 498-4361 or
(714) 962-9836

Jay Malinowski
Director of Publications
Cerritos College, Norwalk
(213) 860-2451 Ext. 215/216

Richard Jacks
215 Riverside Avenue
Newport Beach, California 92663
(714) 645-1550

**Education**

**1995-2000**
California State University Chico
BA Communication Design
emphasis in graphic design

**1999-2000**
VP of Designers in Progress
a design club that involved the
organization of studio tours,
guest speakers and other events

**Work Experience**

**2001-present**
Winslow Press
design of logo and
marketing materials

**2000-2001**
Associated Students Bookstore
design and production of print
advertisements and signage

**1998-2000**
Union Graphics
design and production of
posters and identity systems

**Michael Delgado**
2252 Mariposa Avenue
Chico, CA 95926
530.893.2590
mpd1233@hotmail.com

**Education**

Received a B.A. in Visual Communication with an emphasis in Graphic Design from California State University, Chico in May 1999.

Course work included:
Ad Design, Copywriting, Corporate Identity, Environmental Graphics, Illustration, Letterforms, Packaging, Photography, Publication Design, Typography, and Web Design.

Skills acquired in course work:
Computer experience with Macromedia Freehand, Macromedia Dreamweaver, QuarkXPress, Adobe PageMaker, Adobe Photoshop and Adobe Illustrator.

**Activities / Achievements**

Best of Show, Logo Design
Best of Show, Packaging,
CSU, Chico Student Show, 1999

Designers In Progress, member, 1997-1999

CSU, Chico Dean's List, Fall 1998

Dedicated Designer Award, The Orion, 1998

Envision 22 Poster Competition, competitor, 1998

CSU, Chico Student Show, Competitor, 1998

**Experience**

School of Graduate and International Programs, CSU, Chico, Chico CA
Spring. 1999
Designer

The Orion, Chico, CA
Fall 1998-Spring. 1999
Ad designer

Allen & O'hara Properties, Chico, CA
1992-1997
Desk Attendant / Maintenance

Pleasant Valley Senior High School, Chico, CA
1992-1996
Freshman Boys' Basketball Coach. Assistant Director of Viking Classic.

**Personal**

DOB: 7/19/74

Goal: To obtain a position where I can further my knowledge and skills in the graphic design field.

Interests: Sports in general, Golf, Music and Audio Electronics.

**References**

Available on request.

Masa Uehara
17973 Tyler Foote Road
Nevada City, CA 95959
916 • 292 • 3557

# M A S A

## EDUCATION

1991-1993. California State University, Chico, Graphic Design, Graduate Studies: Corporate Identity, Package Design, Publication Design, Advertising Design, Typography

1992. Elected to Phi Kappa Phi, scholastic honorary society

1990. U.C. Davis Extension, Certificate Program in Graphic Design

Graduate Study in English Literature, Ochanomizu Women's College, Tokyo, Japan

B.A. and Graduate Study in English Literature, Kobe University, Japan

## EXPERIENCE

1992-1993. Internship, Instructional Media Center, CSU, Chico: Client consultation, ideation, and concept sketches through electronic prepress for posters, brochures, newsletters, invitations, and signage

1991-1992. LeeAnn Brook Design, Nevada City, CA: Conventional and electronic production and collaborative design of brochures, packages, logos, ads, annual reports, posters, and business systems

1990- Masa Uehara Design: Design and electronic prepress for small business clients in Grass Valley, Nevada City, Yuba City, Chico, and Sacramento, including corporate identities, business systems, publications, and signage

## AWARDS

Logo Design Competition, Endangered Plants Program, California Dept. of Fish & Game, Second place, 1992

Juried Student Design Competition, CSU, Chico
1992: Best in Trademarks, Best in Publication Design, Best in Business Systems
1991: Second in Typography

## MEMBERSHIPS

Art Directors and Artists Club, Sacramento, CA

Designers in Progress, CSU, Chico, CA

Nevada County Designers' Network

## SKILLS

Computer:
QuarkXpress
Adobe Photoshop
Aldus FreeHand
Adobe Illustrator
PageMaker
Microsoft Word

Languages: Bilingual. Japanese, native speaker English, 25 years

Calligraphy:
Japanese and Chinese

References on request

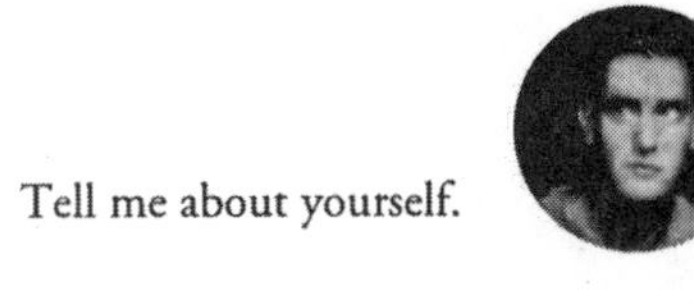

Q. Tell me about yourself.

A. Well, my name is Brian Steele... I am six foot five, a towering willow of a man. Yeah, I guess you could say I have a sense of humor about it. I went to Chico State, and got a BA in Communication Design. Some of the classes I took were, let's see, ad design, corporate identity, typography, and letterforms. I won a few design awards while I was there.

Q. What about the juicy stuff?

A. Oh, you want to know about that. Most recently I worked as an intern for a local design firm, MC2. And before that I had an internship at The News & Review, a local weekly, as an illustrator. I even worked at the El Rey theater, and did their in-house graphics, though it wasn't exactly a payoff for scraping gum off seats.

Brian A

Q. What are your Mac skills?

A. At MC2 I expanded my computer know-how, I guess you could say I know Illustrator, Quark, Freehand, Photoshop, and Microsoft Word.

Q. How about your free time?

A. I like to run hoops, you know basketball. I like to fish, and I have just taken up golfing. I am an avid reader of trade periodicals like CA, and Ad Week. In school I was a member of Designers in Progress, and I volunteered at a food service for homeless people.

Steele

Q. If I had a crystal ball, what would it tell me about your future?

A. Well I suppose it would show me working in a fast paced environment, working closely with people to solve problems in a collaborative effort. I'd probably have my sleeves rolled up, and a smile on my face, cuz that's what I like to do.

Please address questions or comments to: Brian A. Steele 239 Lennox Ave. Menlo Park, CA 94025 tel.415.322.7880 fax.415.322.7848

# MARK HAUSLER SOARS

This resume can fly. Or make a hat. Or start a campfire. But if you need a down to earth designer, read it before you soak up that spilled coffee.

Stratospheric education from California State University, Chico. B.A. in Visual Communications, 1986. Dean's Honor List 1985-1986. Courses include corporate identity, ad design, environmental graphics, illustration, photography, video graphics, and publication design. Also attended San Jose State University. Studied graphic design, drawing and painting. Other significant communication courses include advertising copywriting, scriptwriting and journalism.

Terrestrial experience includes one-on-one client contact solving a variety of communication problems. Created posters, bookcovers, editorial illustration, T-shirts and signs. Interned at the award-winning weekly, *Chico News & Review.* Delivered editorial and advertising assignments. Active in Designers In Progress student design club. Attended the 1986 AIGA Computer Graphics Symposium and exhibited in student art and juried design shows.

Portfolio ready for takeoff. Why not take a few minutes to look at it? Call me at 916 *894 6678* or 415 *324 2271* or write to 56 St. Francis Drive, Chico, CA 95926.

CORINNE HAIG PEZZETTI • 41 TOM POLK CIRCLE • CHICO, CA 95926 • 916-343-9882

## WORK EXPERIENCE

**FREELANCE DESIGNER:** Design business cards, logos, menus, newspaper ads, tee shirts, and labels. Clients include: Zoftware & Associates, Safeway, Andy Enterprises, SMS Screenprinters, KFM Radio, Campus Cafe, Larkin Automotive, and Poppin' Kettle. November 1992-Present. • **PROMOTIONAL DESIGNER:** Management Department, CSU, Chico. Designed all promotional material for Americans with Disabilities Act Conference. Fall 1992. • **DESIGN ASSISTANT:** 2nd Street Graphics, Chico, CA. Designed brochures, logos, business systems, mechanicals, and operated process camera. Summer 1991. • **PUBLICITY STAFF:** Independent Living Services, Chico, CA. Worked on *Independent Life* newsletter, utilized photography and videography skills, wrote articles, and designed brochures. Spring 1991. • **FLORAL MANAGER:** Safeway Stores, Chico, CA. Floral design, display and inventory skills were performed. February 1986-September 1989.

## MAC

Fluent with following **SOFTWARE:** FreeHand, PageMaker, QuarkXPress, Photoshop and Illustrator. Professional training on the AGFA Select Set 5000 Image Setter.

## EDUCATION

*Bachelor of Arts,* Visual Communications; *Minor,* Business Administration; CSU, Chico 1993. **DESIGN:** Typography, Publication design, Corporate Identity, Packaging, Reprographics, Computer Graphics, Ad Copywriting, Script Writing and Graphic Visualization. • **BUSINESS:** Marketing, Advertising, Consumer Behavior, Management, Accounting and Finance. • **GPA:** 3.4 of 4.0, Honors Program and Dean's List.

## ACTIVITIES

**CONFERENCES:** San Francisco Ad Club Career Day, 1993; Envision 17, 18, & 19, Sacramento, CA; Seybold 1992, San Francisco CA • **MEMBERSHIPS:** Golden Key National Honor Society, Designers in Progress, Art Directors of Sacramento, and American Institute of Graphic Arts • **AWARDS:** Honorable Mention, Annual Student Design Show, CSU Chico, 1992 • **TRAVEL:** Exchange student, Japan.

*RUTH IRENE SANTER*

**Resume**

38 Usonia Road
Pleasantville
New York 10570
914.769.0630

*WORK EXPERIENCE*

**87 88 Graphic designer**
Instructional Media Center, California State University, Chico
publication design for CSU, Chico departments –
individual responsibility for project development stressed, from client contact through production – extensive experience with Pagemaker, Adobe Illustrator, Superpaint, etc., on Apple Macintosh computers

**86 Production artist**
Sacramento, California
Cal Central Press, Communication Design, Gwen Amos Design, See Design

**85 Production artist**
The Galliard Organization, New York City
production, some design work, administrative duties; vendor contact, billing and client contact

*EDUCATION & INTERNSHIPS*

**88 California State University, Chico**
expected M.A. Interdisciplinary Study: Graphic Design & Art
typography, publication design, corporate identification, printmaking, computer art GPA – 3.9
Assistant Art Director – *Impulse* magazine workshop
Associated Students Marketing Division – design internship; computer design, posters

**84 Pratt Graphics Center, New York City**
silkscreen, etching

**82 Yale University**
B.A. Fine Art
printmaking, painting, drawing, photography, video, art history, literature, Spanish, biology

*AWARDS & HONORS*

**88 Juried Student Design Show, CSU, Chico**
1st place poster design
1st place publication design
1st place corporate systems

**Chico Ad Club logo design competition**
cash award

**Mrs. B's logo design competition**
cash award

**87 National Association of Campus Activities Conference**
1st place one color poster

**Association of College Unions International Competition**
1st place one color poster

**Phi Kappa Phi honor society**

*PORTFOLIO & REFERENCES ON REQUEST*

**Craig B. Frazier**
22 years of age
Excellent health
408 Ivy St. #6 (916) 345-3934
Chico, CA 95926
Alternate address
670 Vernon St. #203 (415) 428-1930
Oakland, CA 94610

**Education**
Bachelor of Arts, CSU Chico, 8/1/78
Visual Communications, G.P.A. 3.68
Emphasis of study
Art
Corporate identity
Creative problem solving
Environmental design
Illustration
Magazine production
Packaging
Photography
Television graphics
Typography

**Experience**
Internship, Campus graphics
CSU Chico, 9/1/77 - 12/20/77
Freelance illustration, Image Group
Chico, 12/1/77 - present

**Memberships/Distinctions**
Member of ADAC, Sacramento
Honor Award
Envision 4 student show
Three Honor Awards,
CSUC student show 1978
References furnished upon request

# shane dunne

## Education

California State University, Chico
Major in Communications, Emphasis in Graphic Design
Expected graduation in May 1998

## Design Experience

- Editorial design for the award winning school paper, The Orion
- Passed portfolio review for entry into the graphic design program
- Have had photographs displayed in juried show
- Proficient in: Adobe Illustrator 6.0, Adobe Photoshop 3.0, Quark Xpress, Pagemaker, Microsoft Word, Painter

## Employment

### The Orion Chico, CA

- Designed "News" section one semester
- Designed "Dimensions" section one semester
- Did layouts from beginning to end
- Created illustrations/ layouts for weekly articles

### Landlocked Surf Co Chico, CA

- "Snowboard guy"
- Help customers
- Unpacked Shipments
- Maintained a pleasant environment

### Sugar Bowl Ski Reort Norden, CA

- Sold lift tickets, equipment rentals and lessons
- Helped people figure out what they needed to rent or buy
- Handled thousands of dollars a day

### Boreal Ski Area Truckee, CA

- Taught snowboarding to all age groups
- Helped people solve technique problems

## Interests

**snowboarding, Martial Arts drawing, Painting, Photography Juggling, hiking, Tennis, Music**

Shane Dunne
630 Esplanalde #2
Chico,CA 95926
(916) 342-2870

814 Rancheria #A
Chico Ca. 95926
530-892-8799

# Gary A Baugh

**Goal** An internship or part-time position while completing a degree in Graphic Design.

**Education** Bachelor of Arts; Graphic Design, CSU Chico.
*Graduation, December 2000*

1982–84 Memphis State University, Fine Arts Major.

## Work Experience

◆ **1990–97 Graphic Artist for Langston Bag Co., multiwall packaging**
Part of a three man graphics team that implemented the transition from traditional Pre-press production methods to digital technology. Macintosh based programs; Photoshop 5.02, Illustrator 8.0, QuarkXPress. A high volume, fast paced atmosphere. Responsible for complete color separated production negatives for Flexo plates.

◆ **1986–90 Silkscreen Department head for ASI Sign Systems Inc.**
Responsible for printing, scheduling, and job tracking.

◆ **1987–90 Connie Hendrix & Associates Advertising**
Freelance work on agency projects: including Maybeline cosmetics and Thompson Formby's. Constructing 3-dimensional pieces for photo spreads.

◆ **1988–90 Architectural Presentation Arts.**
Freelance work on architectural models and presentation renderings.

**Awards** 1998–99 Deans list for academic excellence, CSU Chico.

1999 first place CSU campus digital art show.

Delta Artist Society annual art show, Memphis TN.
1993 first place: drawing.
1992 Best of show!
1991 first place, oil painting.

*Portfolio Available*

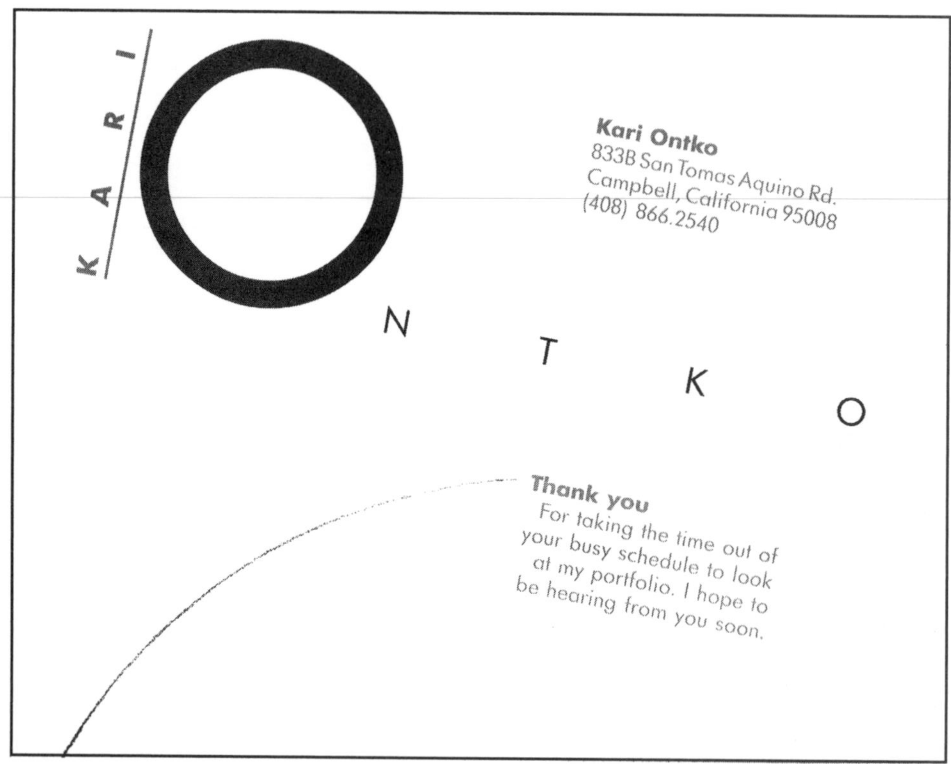
K A R I
N T K O
Kari Ontko
833B San Tomas Aquino Rd.
Campbell, California 95008
(408) 866.2540
Thank you
For taking the time out of
your busy schedule to look
at my portfolio. I hope to
be hearing from you soon.

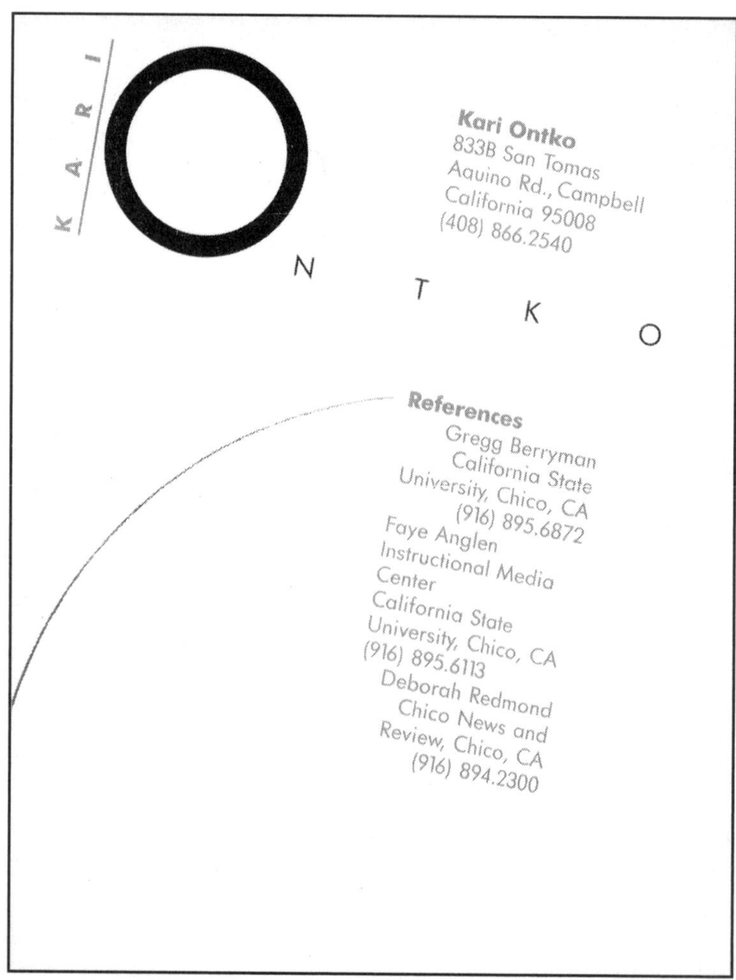
K A R I
N T K O
Kari Ontko
833B San Tomas
Aquino Rd., Campbell
California 95008
(408) 866.2540
References
Gregg Berryman
California State
University, Chico, CA
(916) 895.6872
Faye Anglen
Instructional Media
Center
California State
University, Chico, CA
(916) 895.6113
Deborah Redmond
Chico News and
Review, Chico, CA
(916) 894.2300

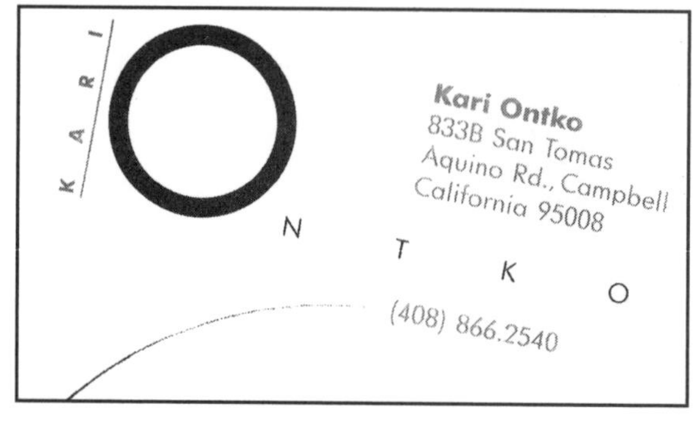
K A R I
N T K O
Kari Ontko
833B San Tomas
Aquino Rd., Campbell
California 95008
(408) 866.2540

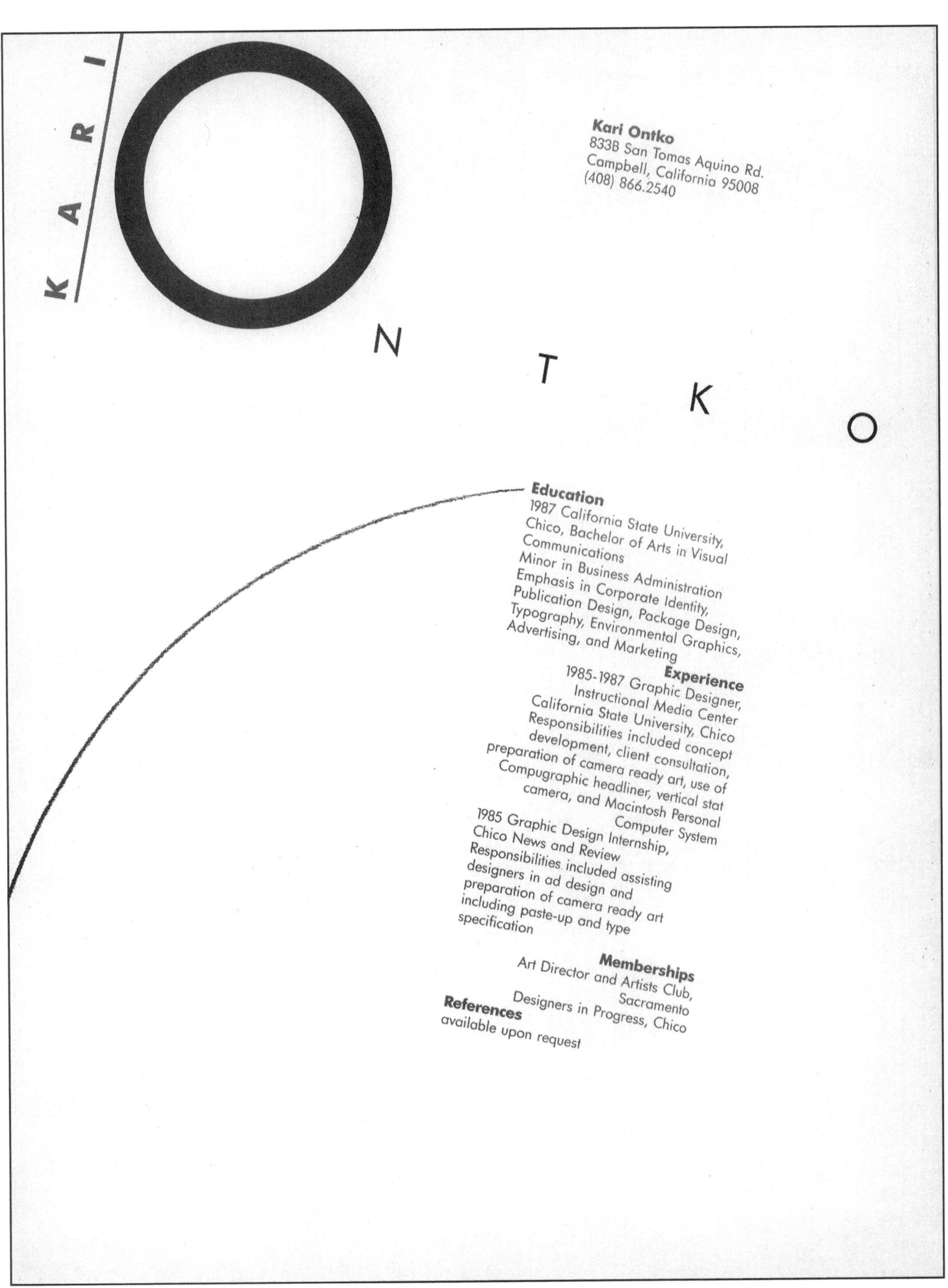

KARI
O N T K O

**Kari Ontko**
833B San Tomas Aquino Rd.
Campbell, California 95008
(408) 866.2540

**Education**
1987 California State University, Chico, Bachelor of Arts in Visual Communications
Minor in Business Administration
Emphasis in Corporate Identity, Publication Design, Package Design, Typography, Environmental Graphics, Advertising, and Marketing

**Experience**
1985-1987 Graphic Designer, Instructional Media Center California State University, Chico
Responsibilities included concept development, client consultation, preparation of camera ready art, use of Compugraphic headliner, vertical stat camera, and Macintosh Personal Computer System

1985 Graphic Design Internship, Chico News and Review
Responsibilities included assisting designers in ad design and preparation of camera ready art including paste-up and type specification

**Memberships**
Art Director and Artists Club, Sacramento
Designers in Progress, Chico

**References**
available upon request

## Education

California State University, Chico
*B.A. Visual Communication*
Modesto College
*General Education*

## Focus

Corporate Identity
Publication
Packaging
Reproduction Graphics
Typography
Graphic Visualization
Advertising Copywriting
Lettering
Design Workshop

## Experience

IMC Graphic Design Student Assistant • CSUC
*Student Intern, Fall 1992*
*Publication, poster, and special events design projects*
Department of Humanities and Fine Arts • CSUC
*Student Intern, Fall 1990*
*Poster design*
Willey Printing Co., Inc.
*Graphic Artist, 1989*
*Mechanical artwork and camera work*

## MacLiteracy

Quark XPress 3.11
Aldus Freehand 3.1
Pagemaker 4.0
Adobe Photoshop

## Awards

Gilbert Paper Student Design Competition
*Commendation award*
Bidwell Mansion T-shirt Design Competition
*1st award*
Modesto College Poster Design Competition
*1st award*
Dean's List, CSUC
*Fall 1992*

## Activities & Workshops

Envision 17 & 18
*Design Conference*
Designers in Progress
*CSUC Design Organization*
*1991,1992*

## References

Gregg Berryman
*Professor, Visual Communication*
*California State University, Chico*
*Office 916.898.6872 • Home 916.343.6800*

Laura Kling
*Art Director, IMC Graphics*
*California State University, Chico*
*Office 916.898.6113 • Home 916.894.5125*

Kevin Cahill
*Professor, Visual Communication*
*California State University, Chico*
*Office 916.898.4776 • Home 916.343.8511*

## Thank You

Thanks for the opportunity to
share my portfolio with you.
Your time was greatly appreciated.
I hope to hear from you soon.

Candy Thompson
209.521.0902

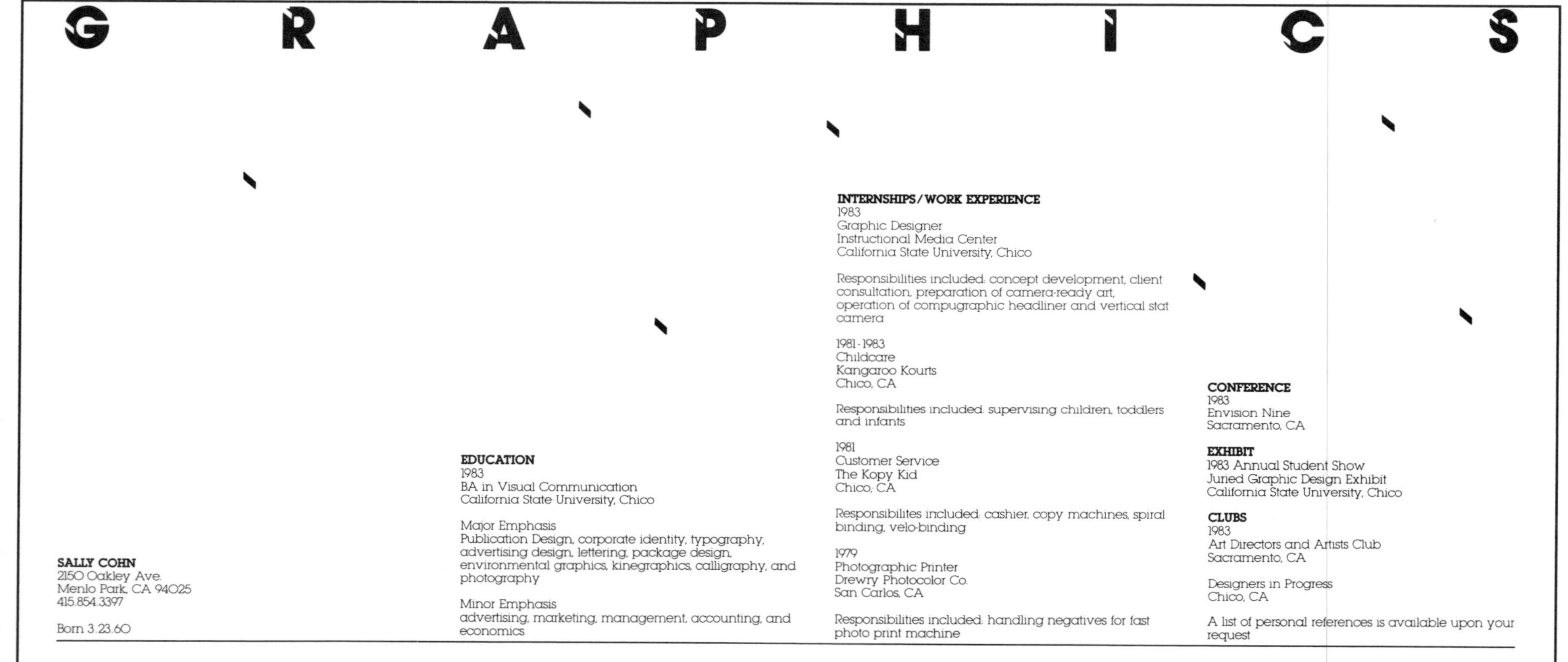

# G R A P H I C S

**SALLY COHN**
2150 Oakley Ave.
Menlo Park, CA 94025
415.854.3397

Born 3.23.60

**EDUCATION**
1983
BA in Visual Communication
California State University, Chico

Major Emphasis
Publication Design, corporate identity, typography, advertising design, lettering, package design, environmental graphics, kinegraphics, calligraphy, and photography

Minor Emphasis
advertising, marketing, management, accounting, and economics

**INTERNSHIPS/WORK EXPERIENCE**
1983
Graphic Designer
Instructional Media Center
California State University, Chico

Responsibilities included: concept development, client consultation, preparation of camera-ready art, operation of compugraphic headliner and vertical stat camera

1981-1983
Childcare
Kangaroo Kourts
Chico, CA

Responsibilities included: supervising children, toddlers and infants

1981
Customer Service
The Kopy Kid
Chico, CA

Responsibilites included: cashier, copy machines, spiral binding, velo-binding

1979
Photographic Printer
Drewry Photocolor Co.
San Carlos, CA

Responsibilities included: handling negatives for fast photo print machine

**CONFERENCE**
1983
Envision Nine
Sacramento, CA

**EXHIBIT**
1983 Annual Student Show
Juried Graphic Design Exhibit
California State University, Chico

**CLUBS**
1983
Art Directors and Artists Club
Sacramento, CA

Designers in Progress
Chico, CA

A list of personal references is available upon your request

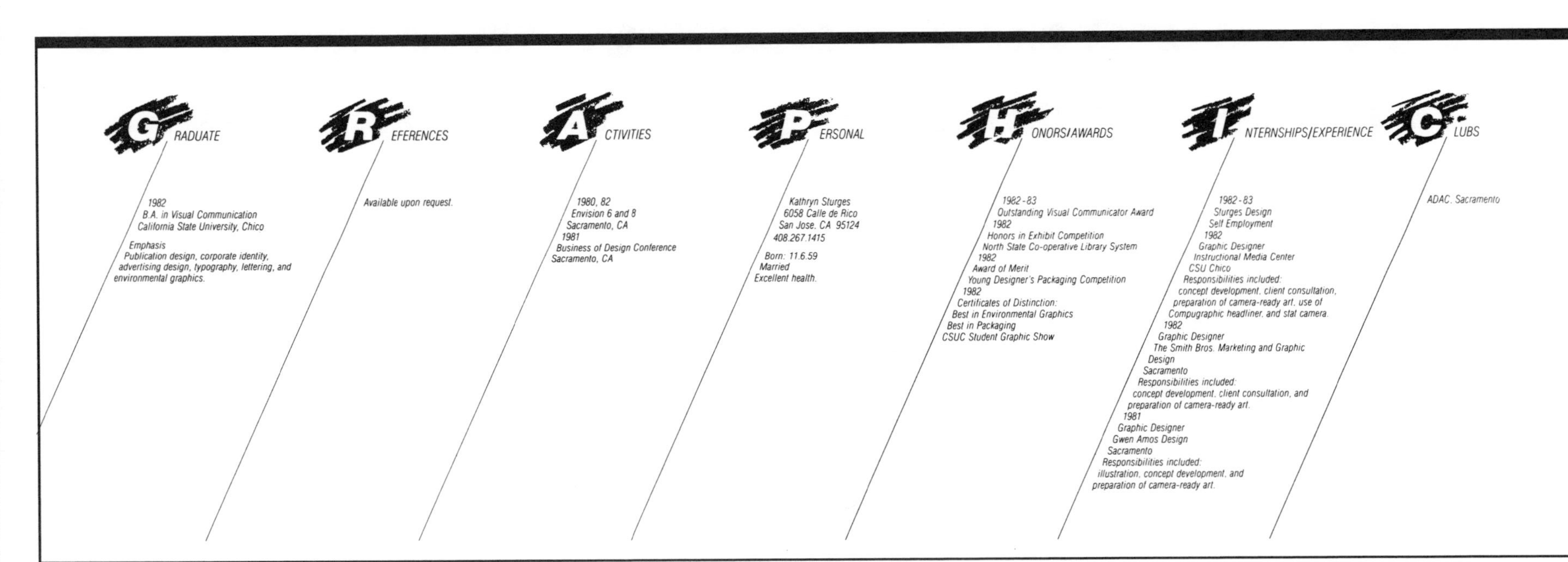

**G**RADUATE

1982
B.A. in Visual Communication
California State University, Chico

Emphasis
Publication design, corporate identity, advertising design, typography, lettering, and environmental graphics.

**R**EFERENCES

Available upon request.

**A**CTIVITIES

1980, 82
Envision 6 and 8
Sacramento, CA
1981
Business of Design Conference
Sacramento, CA

**P**ERSONAL

Kathryn Sturges
6058 Calle de Rico
San Jose, CA 95124
408.267.1415

Born: 11.6.59
Married
Excellent health.

**H**ONORS/AWARDS

1982-83
Outstanding Visual Communicator Award
1982
Honors in Exhibit Competition
North State Co-operative Library System
1982
Award of Merit
Young Designer's Packaging Competition
1982
Certificates of Distinction:
Best in Environmental Graphics
Best in Packaging
CSUC Student Graphic Show

**I**NTERNSHIPS/EXPERIENCE

1982-83
Sturges Design
Self Employment
1982
Graphic Designer
Instructional Media Center
CSU Chico
Responsibilities included:
concept development, client consultation, preparation of camera-ready art, use of Compugraphic headliner, and stat camera.
1982
Graphic Designer
The Smith Bros. Marketing and Graphic Design
Sacramento
Responsibilities included:
concept development, client consultation, and preparation of camera-ready art.
1981
Graphic Designer
Gwen Amos Design
Sacramento
Responsibilities included:
illustration, concept development, and preparation of camera-ready art.

**C**LUBS

ADAC, Sacramento

## *ALEX SORGER*
25 Lerida Court
Portola Valley, CA 94025
✆**415.854.6965**

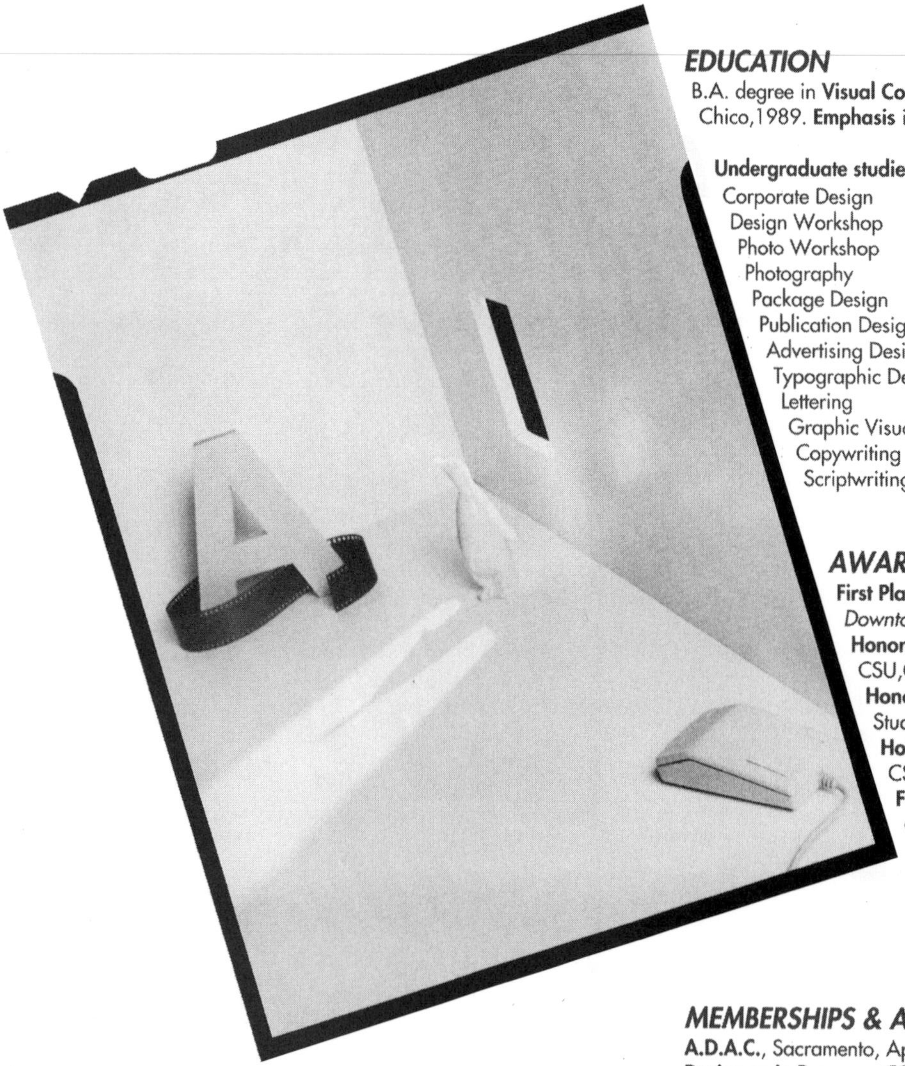

## *EDUCATION*
B.A. degree in **Visual Communications**. California State University, Chico,1989. **Emphasis** in Graphic Design and Photography.

**Undergraduate studies:**
Corporate Design
Design Workshop
Photo Workshop
Photography
Package Design
Publication Design
Advertising Design
Typographic Design
Lettering
Graphic Visualization
Copywriting
Scriptwriting

## *AWARDS*
**First Place**. Corporate Identity for *Historic Downtown Gridley*. May 1989.
**Honorable Mention**. Publication Cover, CSU,Chico Student Design Show. May 1989.
**Honorable Mention**. Symbol/Logo, CSU,Chico Student Design Show. May 1989.
**Honorable Mention**. Package Design, CSU,Chico Student Design Show. May 1988.
**First Place**. Newspaper Banner Design for *Off the Record*, Chico. March 1988.

## *MEMBERSHIPS & ACTIVITIES*
**A.D.A.C.**, Sacramento, April 1989 to present.
**Designers in Progress**, CSU,Chico. Fall 1987 to Spring 1989.
**Envision Fifteen** Design Conference, Sacramento. May 1989.
**CSU,Chico Ski Club**, President. Fall 1987 to Spring 1989.
**O.A.R.S. Raft Trips**, qualified raft guide. June 1986 to present.

## *EXPERIENCE*
**Internship**. I.M.C. Graphics, Chico. Spring 1989.
Created posters and brochures for campus clients. Designed thumbnails, performed type specification and paste-up for mechanicals, and operated vertical stat camera. Utilized a Macintosh desktop publishing system with the following software programs; Page Maker, Adobe Illustrator, Aldus Freehand and others with laserprinting capabilities.

**Art Director**. *The Orion* campus newspaper, Chico. Fall 1988. Responsibilities include page layout, photo selection and sizing, utilizing a Macintosh desktop publishing system. *The Orion* was awarded first place for Best Overall Design and for the Broadsheet Design categories at the C.I.P.A. convention, San Luis Obispo, March 1988.

**References** and portfolio display available upon request.

## education

1983
Bachelor of Art
Visual Communications;
emphasis in photography
California State University, Chico

Course of Study
Studio lighting/Bank lighting,
Advertising/Product photography,
Portrait photography,
Photojournalism, News and
copywriting, Screenprinting,
and Marketing skills.

## memberships

Women in Communications,
Chico Ca.
Designers in Progress, Chico Ca.
Communications Club, Chico Ca.
Marketing Club, Chico Ca.

## exhibits

1980
CSU Chico Meriam Library.
1979
Fisher Gallery, Chico Ca.
Community display, Chico Ca.
Butte College Campus Center,
Chico Ca.

## experience

1982-1983
Instructional Media Center
CSU Chico
Photographer
Responsibilities include: Working directly with designers to fulfill their photographic needs. Use of high speed film with available light to photograph dramatic events. Photographed and printed for University catalog. Using annual report format in developing brochures for University departments. Standard processing of film and running machine process of E6.

1982-1983
Freelance Photographer
Responsibilities include: Advertising photography, passport and portrait photography.

1980-1982
Meriam Library
CSU Chico
Student Assistant
Responsibilities include: Working with the public. Operation and maintenance of non-print equipment. Use of keyboard computers, and clerical work.

1979-1980
Photojournalist
CSU Chico Record Yearbook

## special projects

1982
Developed a complete slide/tape presentation on the social and psychological effects of Graffiti.

In a group situation developed a major marketing proposal for P.G.E. using multi-media.

1981
Designed and photographed publicity campaign for Phi Kappa Tau fraternity's sheriff candidate.

Wrote, directed and, produced a 10 minute documentary film on the world of the deaf; "A World of Silence."

Researched and wrote an extensive paper on Subliminal Advertising, including visual aids.

1982
Slide Presentation workshop,
Chico Ca.
Color and Pigments, Chico Ca.
1981
Studio Bank Lighting, Chico Ca.
1979
Photo Field Experience, Chico Ca.
Nikon Weekend, San Francisco Ca.
1977
Photo and Sound Company,
San Francisco Ca.

## personal

Julie Schroer
276 East 7th Avenue
Chico, Ca 95926
(916) 342.2127
(916) 891.6534

Portfolio and References available on request.

## *Leslie Flores*

Leslie Flores
935 Bryant Ave.
Chico, CA 95926
916 342 0217

## *Education*

1981
B.A. in Visual Communications
California State University, Chico

1977
Certificate of Completion
The Glen Fishback School
of Photography

## *Job objective*

Position as documentary photographer for publications.

## *Experience*

1982
Pin One On
Photo Pin Business
Co-owner

1977-Present
Freelance Photographer
Chico News & Review

1979-1981
Staff Photographer
Instructional Media Center
CSUC

1977-1978
Photographer
Impulse Magazines
Orion, Student Newspaper
CSUC

## *Awards*

1981, 1979, 1977
Best in Show
1980, 1978
First Place
Silver Dollar Fair, Chico

1980
Honor Award
University/College Designers
Association

1978-1981
7 Honor Awards
CSUC Student Show

## *Exhibits*

1982
Retrospective
LaSalles Restaurant, Chico

1981, 1978
Learning Center, CSUC

1980
Creative Arts Center, Chico

1977
Women's Center, Chico

## *Workshops*

1982
Tahoe Photographic Workshop
Documentary
Mary Ellen Mark

1982
Maple House Photography Lectures
Fremont, CA

1981
The Friends of Photography
Members Workshop
Carmel, CA

## *Memberships*

The Friends of Photography, Carmel
Sacramento Art Directors Club
Designers in Progress, Chico

References upon request

*Self-Portrait*
*1982*

*Laguna Beach Ladies*
*1981*

AWARDS

*1981*
*Outstanding Visual Communicator Award*
*California State University, Chico*

*1981*
*Honorable Mention*
*Camera Portfolio Magazine*

*1979, 1980, 1981*
*Best in Show, Photography*
*CSU-Chico Student*
*Visual Communication Annual*

*1979, 1980, 1981*
*5 Honor Awards*
*CSU-Chico Student*
*Visual Communication Annual*

*1980*
*Best in Show, Photography*
*Silver Dollar Regional Fair*
*Chico, CA*

EXHIBITIONS

*1982*
*La Salles Restaurant*
*Chico, CA*

*1982*
*Bell Camera, Inc.*
*Chico, CA*

*1981*
*Omni Arts Show*
*Chico, CA*

*1978, 1981*
*Meriam Library, CSU-Chico*
*Chico, CA*

*1980*
*Creative Arts Center*
*Chico, CA*

*1977*
*Women's Center Gallery*
*Chico, CA*

*1977*
*Bell Memorial Union, CSU-Chico*
*Chico, CA*

WORKSHOPS/CONFERENCES

*1982*
*Tahoe Photographic Workshop*
*Documentary*
*Mary Ellen Mark*

*1978, 1979, 1980, 1981, 1982*
*Envision/Design Conferences*
*Sacramento, CA*

*1982*
*Maple House Photography Lectures*
*Fremont, CA*

*1981*
*The Friends of Photography*
*Members' Workshop*
*Carmel, CA*

*1975*
*Aperture '75/Photography Conference*
*Chico, CA*

*References upon request*

*Pool Chairs*
*1979*

EDUCATION

*1981*
*Bachelor of Arts Degree*
*Visual Communications*
*California State University, Chico*

*1977*
*Certificate of Achievement*
*The Glen Fishback School*
*of Photography*
*Sacramento, CA*

EXPERIENCE

*1978-1982*
*Staff Photographer*
*University Relations/Alumni Office*
*California State University, Chico*

*Responsibilities included photography for alumni newspaper, annual reports, university catalogs, brochures, and publicity releases.*

*1977-present*
*Freelance Photographer*
*Publication, documentary, portrait, brochure, catalog, and advertising photography.*
*Multimedia slide presentations.*

*1982-present*
*Pin One On*
*Photo Pin Business*
*Co-Owner*

*1977-1978*
*Photographer*
*Activities Office*
*California State University, Chico*

*Responsibilities included publicity photographs for sporting events, drama productions, and art exhibitions.*

*1978, 1981, 1982*
*Photographer*
*Impulse Magazine*
*California State University, Chico*

MEMBERSHIPS

*Art Directors and Artists Club*
*Sacramento, CA*

*The Friends of Photography*
*Carmel, CA*

*Women in Communications, Inc.*
*National Chapter*
*Chico Chapter*

*Designers in Progress*
*Chico, CA*

*Legs*
*1982*

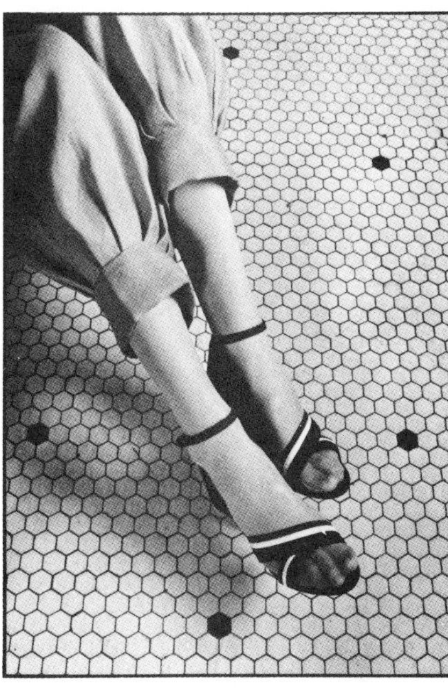

can

can do.

**Candido Salinas III**

*Graphic Design*
*986 Salem*
*Chico, California 95928*
*916 894-7271*

**education:**

*1986 B.A. Visual Communications*
*Minor: Graphic Arts Technology/Art*
*California State University, Chico*

**course of study:**

*Publication Design*
*Corporate Identity*
*Environmental Graphics*
*Design Workshop*
*Package Design*
*Typography*
*Lettering*
*Illustration*
*Reprographics*
*Copy Preparation*
*Process Camera*
*Airbrush Painting*
*Screen Printing*

**experience:**

*1985-86 3-D Graphic Designer*
*3-D Design Group*

*A freelance design studio. Projects included company identities, posters, brochures, and outdoor advertising.*

*1984-85 Graphic Designer*
***Instructional Media Center***
***California State University, Chico***

*Responsibilities included the design and production of graphic media for the University including posters, brochures, and flyers.*

*1981-85 Graphic Designer*
***Technical Information Department***
***Naval Weapons Center***
***China Lake, California***

*Responsibilities included the design and execution of classified government information for use in technical briefings.*

**activities/memberships:**

***1983-86 Designers in Progress***
*California State University, Chico*

***1984-86 Art Directors and Artists Club***
*Sacramento, California*

***1985-86 Envision Conferences 11, 12***
*Sacramento, California*

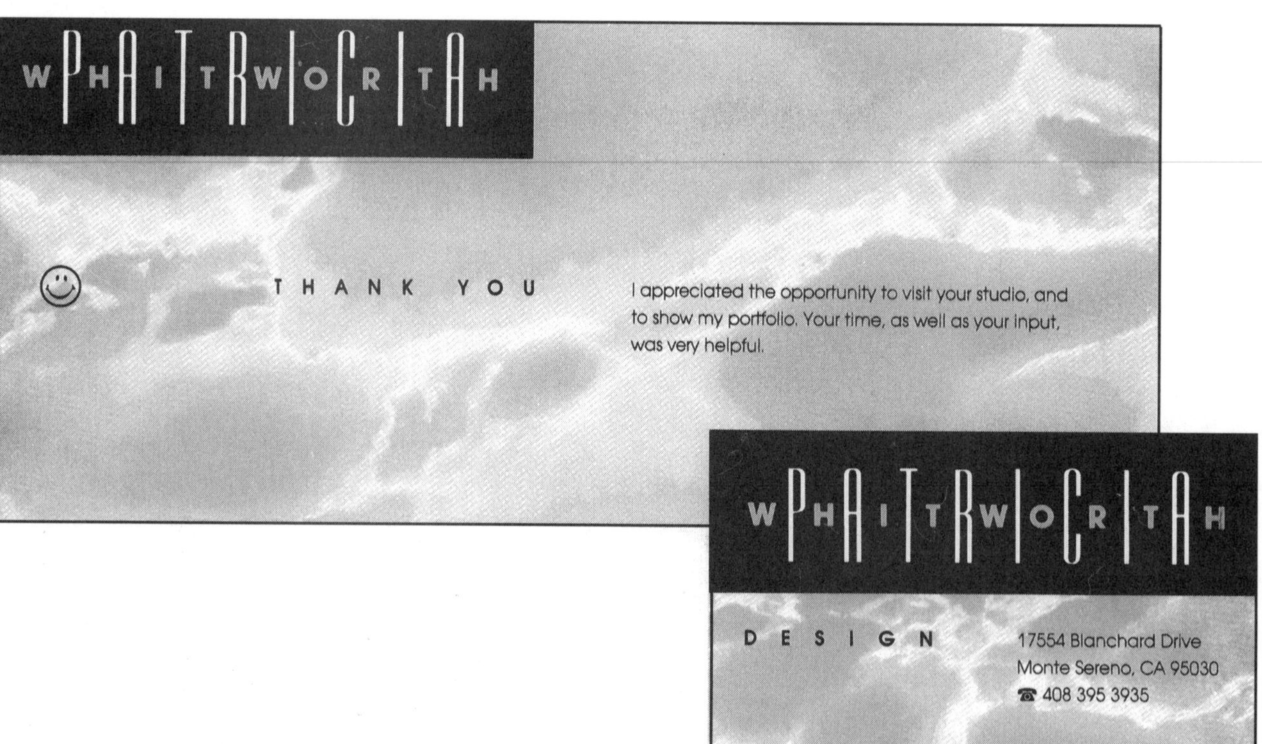

PATRICIA WHITWORTH

THANK YOU

I appreciated the opportunity to visit your studio, and to show my portfolio. Your time, as well as your input, was very helpful.

PATRICIA WHITWORTH

DESIGN

17554 Blanchard Drive
Monte Sereno, CA 95030
☎ 408 395 3935

PATRICIA WHITWORTH

PERSONAL

17554 Blanchard Drive
Monte Sereno, CA 95030
☎ 408 395 3935

REFERENCES

David Boring - Owner of Never Boring Design Associates; Modesto, California.
☎ 209 526 9136 Office

Gregg Berryman - Professor of Graphic Design; C.S.U. Chico, California.
☎ 916 895 6872 Office
☎ 916 343 6500 Home

Carole Montgomery - Freelance Graphic Designer and Instructor; Paradise, California.
☎ 916 877 5124 Home

# PATRICIA WHITWORTH

## PERSONAL

17554 Blanchard Drive
Monte Sereno, CA 95030
☎ 408 395 3935

## EXPERIENCE

1988 to 1990 Never Boring Design Associates, Modesto; Graphic Designer. Projects included logos, identity systems, packaging, posters, brochures, advertisements, displays, billboards, and promotional folders. Worked directly with clients. Responsibilities included writing contracts, designing for client approval, producing camera ready art, and supervision of printing.

1987 Center for Regional and Continuing Education, C.S.U. Chico; Graphic Designer. Projects included designing flyers, brochures and posters. Started as a design intern assisting Carole Montgomery and was hired on after six months until graduation.

## EDUCATION

1987 California State University, Chico; Received a Bachelor of Fine Art in Communication Design and a Minor in Art Studio.

1982 - 1984 San Jose State University; Majored in Fine Art with an emphasis on graphic design.

## EMPHASIS

Publication Design, Package Design, Computer Graphics, Reproduction Graphics, Typography, Graphic Visualization, Ad Copywriting, Airbrush, Printmaking, Illustration, and Silkscreen.

## ACTIVITIES

1986 - 1987 Member of Designers in Progress, C.S.U. Chico.

1984 - 1985 Active Member of Chi Omega Sorority, San Jose State University.

1982 - 1984 Volunteer Swim Instructor for Friends Outside, San Jose.

References on request.

Mini-Portfolio
Inside

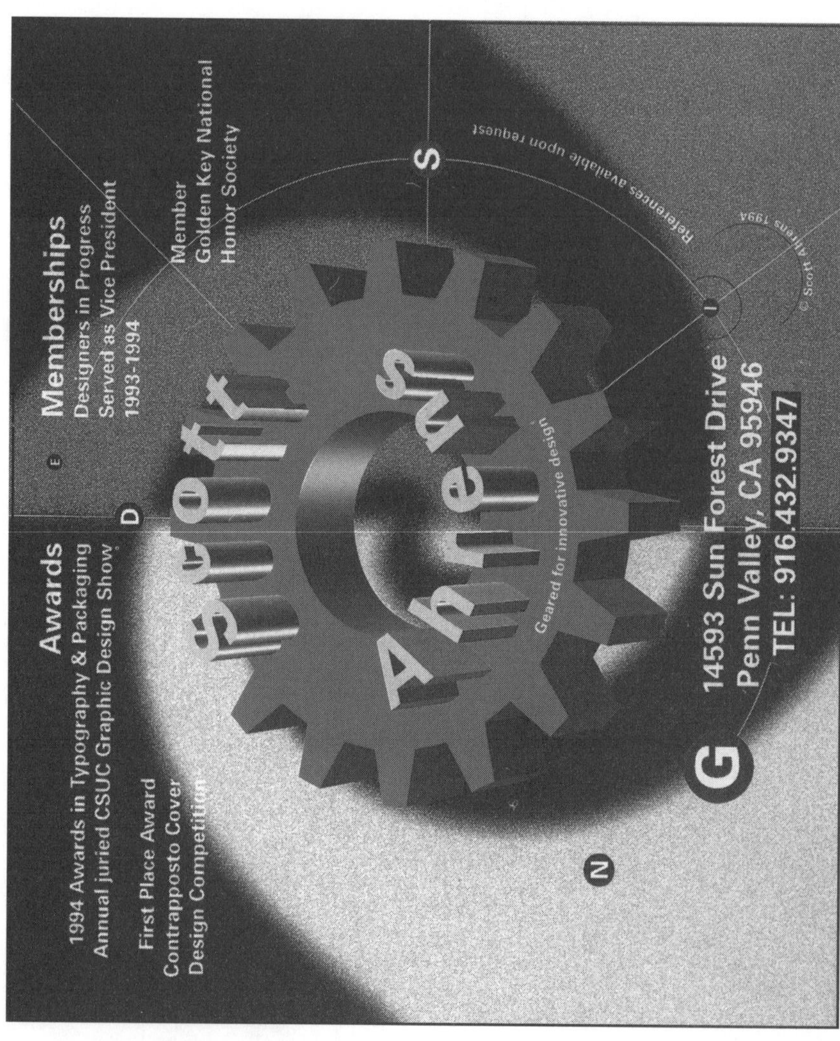
Awards
1994 Awards in Typography & Packaging
Annual juried CSUC Graphic Design Show
First Place Award
Contrapposto Cover
Design Competition
Memberships
Designers in Progress
Served as Vice President
1993-1994
Member
Golden Key National
Honor Society
Geared for innovative design
References available upon request
© Scott Ahrens 1994
14593 Sun Forest Drive
Penn Valley, CA 95946
TEL: 916.432.9347

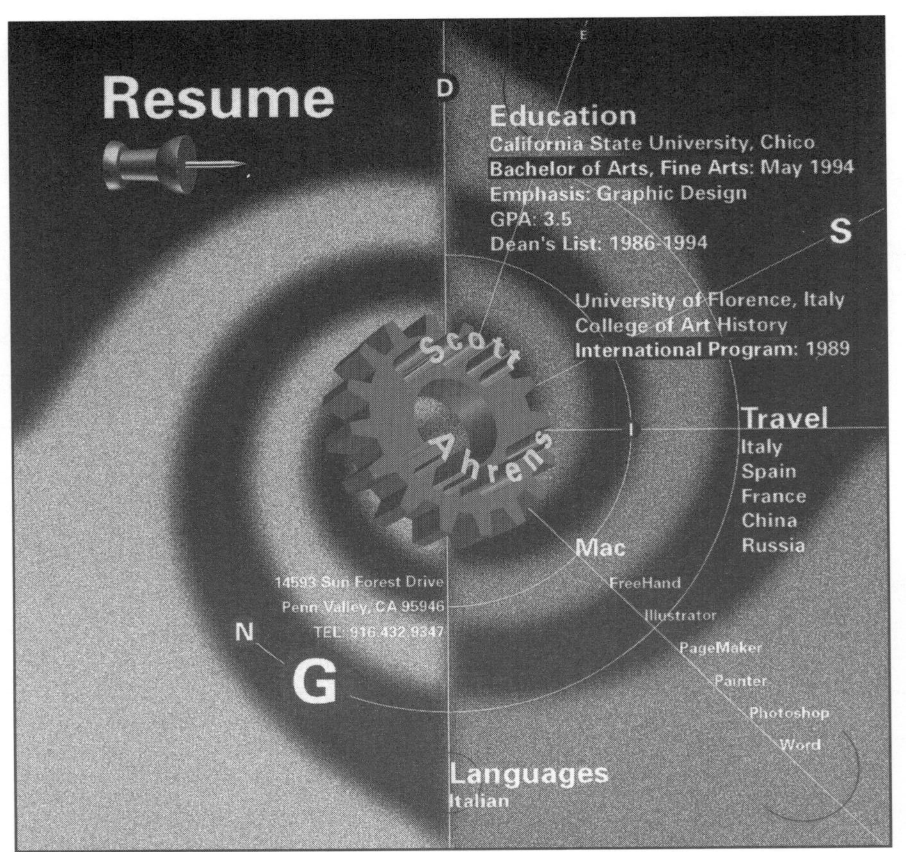
Resume
D
E
Education
California State University, Chico
Bachelor of Arts, Fine Arts: May 1994
Emphasis: Graphic Design
GPA: 3.5
Dean's List: 1986-1994
S
University of Florence, Italy
College of Art History
International Program: 1989
Scott
Ahrens
I
Travel
Italy
Spain
France
China
Russia
Mac
FreeHand
Illustrator
PageMaker
Painter
Photoshop
Word
14593 Sun Forest Drive
Penn Valley, CA 95946
TEL: 916.432.9347
N
G
Languages
Italian

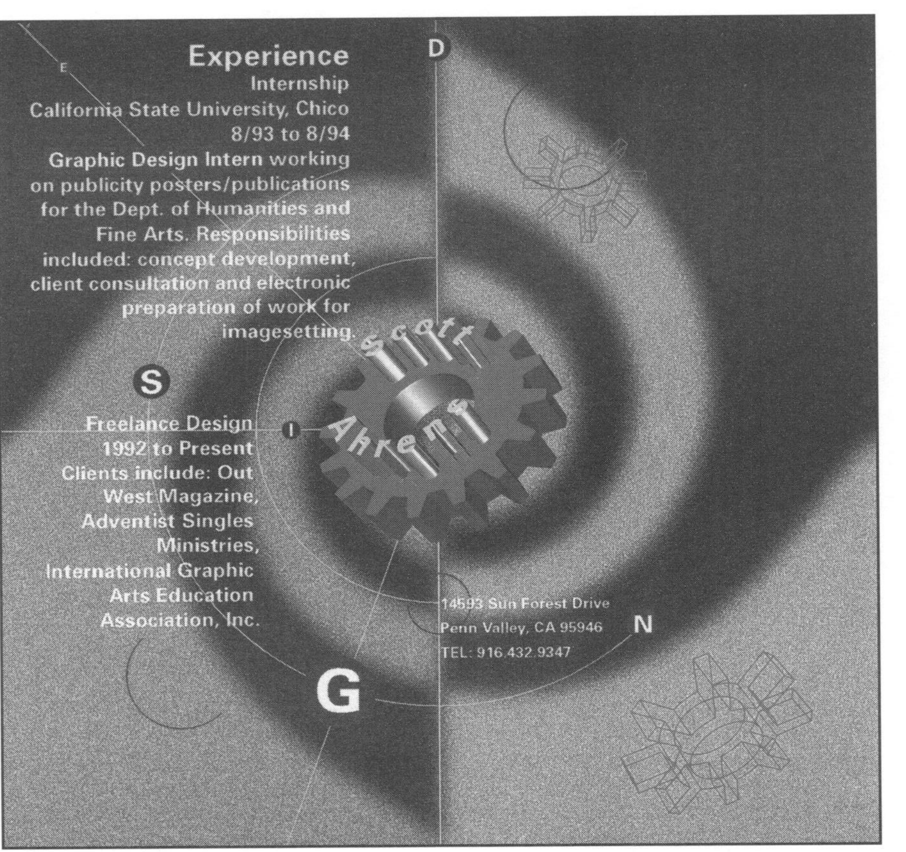
E
Experience
Internship
California State University, Chico
8/93 to 8/94
Graphic Design Intern working
on publicity posters/publications
for the Dept. of Humanities and
Fine Arts. Responsibilities
included: concept development,
client consultation and electronic
preparation of work for
imagesetting.
D
Scott
Ahrens
S
I
Freelance Design
1992 to Present
Clients include: Out
West Magazine,
Adventist Singles
Ministries,
International Graphic
Arts Education
Association, Inc.
14593 Sun Forest Drive
Penn Valley, CA 95946
TEL: 916.432.9347
N
G

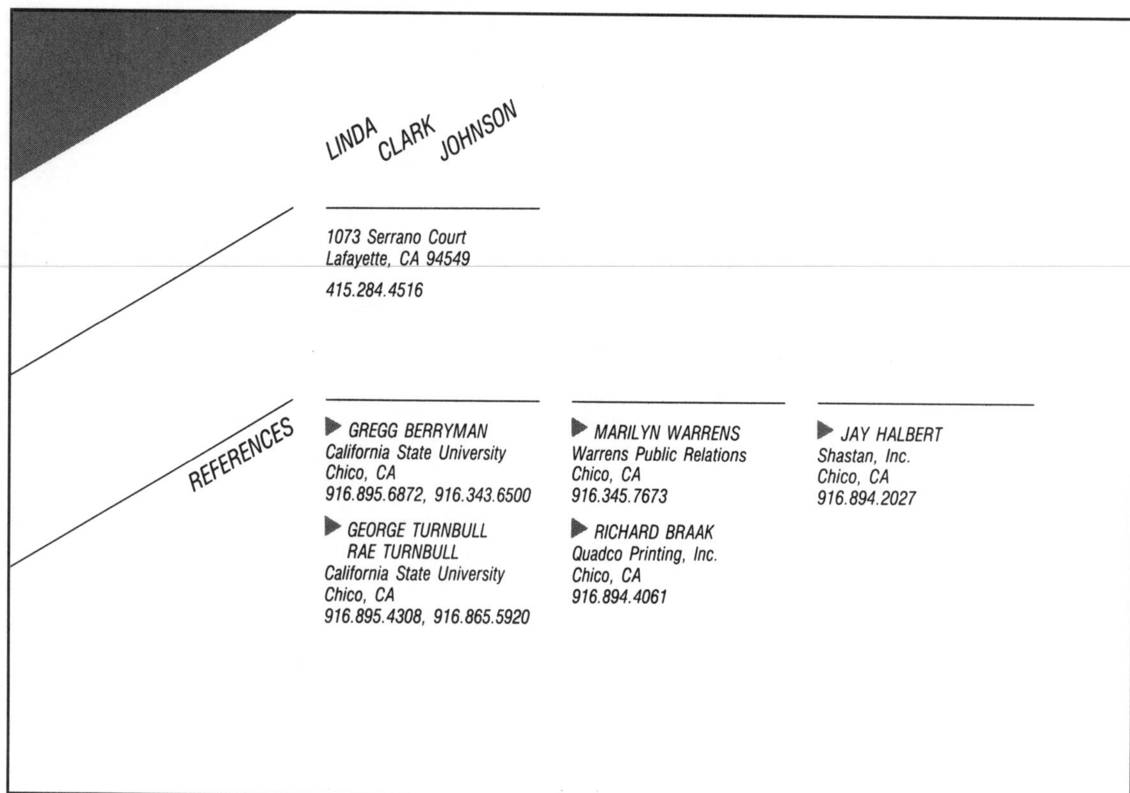
LINDA CLARK JOHNSON
1073 Serrano Court
Lafayette, CA 94549
415.284.4516
REFERENCES
GREGG BERRYMAN
California State University
Chico, CA
916.895.6872, 916.343.6500
GEORGE TURNBULL
RAE TURNBULL
California State University
Chico, CA
916.895.4308, 916.865.5920
MARILYN WARRENS
Warrens Public Relations
Chico, CA
916.345.7673
RICHARD BRAAK
Quadco Printing, Inc.
Chico, CA
916.894.4061
JAY HALBERT
Shastan, Inc.
Chico, CA
916.894.2027

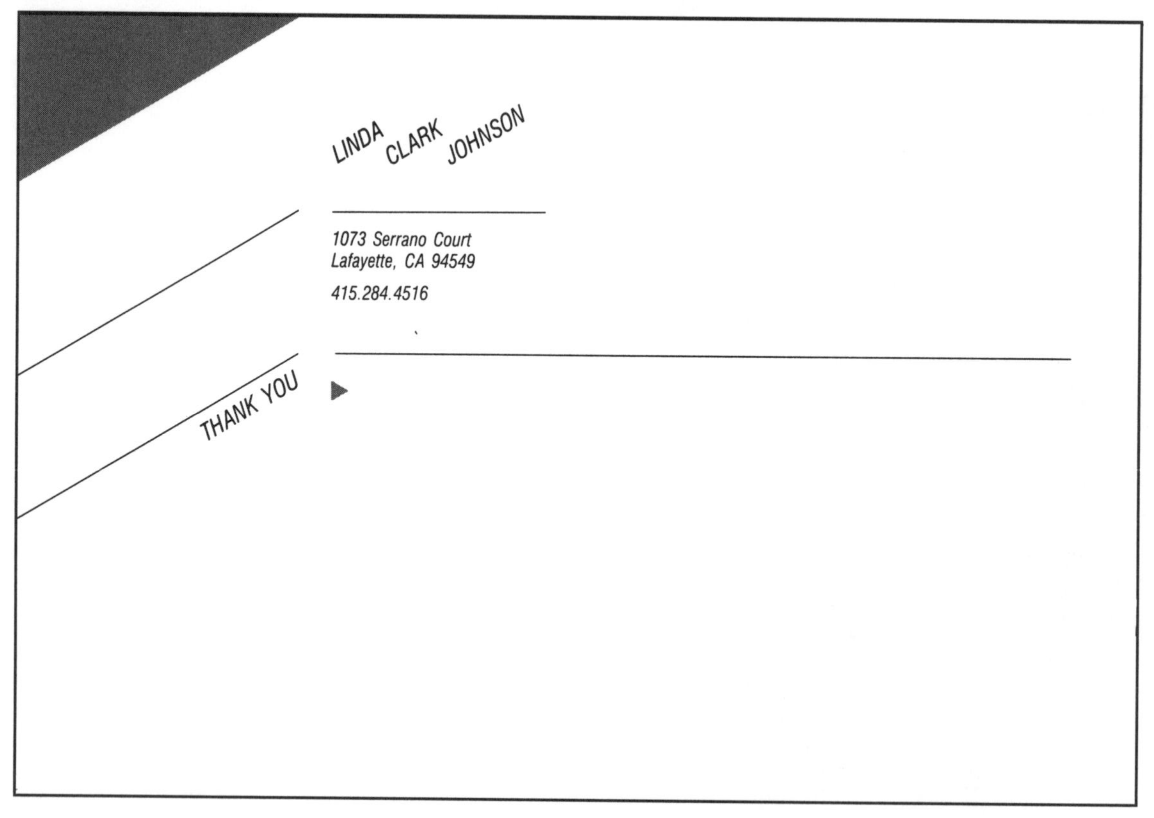
LINDA CLARK JOHNSON
1073 Serrano Court
Lafayette, CA 94549
415.284.4516
THANK YOU

LINDA CLARK JOHNSON

1073 Serrano Court
Lafayette, CA 94549
415.284.4516

| | WORK EXPERIENCE | EDUCATION | INTERNSHIPS | AWARDS | MEMBERSHIPS |
|---|---|---|---|---|---|
| 1983 | ▶ GRAPHIC DESIGNER<br>Clark Design & Illustration<br>Chico, CA<br>1982 to 1983<br>Consulting graphic designer and illustrator for university, public relations firm, corporations, and other design studios.<br>▶ LITHOGRAPHIC STRIPPER<br>Quadco Printing, Inc.<br>Chico, CA<br>1978 to 1983<br>Responsible for all complex film assembly, including four color process, in quality commercial printing company. Also worked in paste-up, camera, proofing, and platemaking departments. | ▶ | ▶ | ▶ ANNUAL DESIGN SHOW<br>California State University<br>Chico, CA<br>1983<br>Honor Award: Calligraphy | ▶ ART DIRECTORS & ARTISTS CLUB<br>Sacramento, CA<br>1979 to present |
| 1982 | ▶ | ▶ CALIFORNIA STATE UNIVERSITY, CHICO<br>Chico, CA<br>1979 to 1982<br>Course work in graphic design; including publication design, corporate identity, typography, illustration, calligraphy, photography, packaging, and creative problem solving. | ▶ GRAPHIC DESIGNER<br>Art Department<br>California State University<br>Chico, CA<br>1981 to 1982<br>Designed publicity posters for University Art Gallery.<br>▶ ART DIRECTOR<br>Impulse Magazine<br>California State University<br>Chico, CA<br>1982<br>Art direction, scheduling, and quality control for an annual student magazine. | ▶ ANNUAL DESIGN SHOW<br>California State University<br>Chico, CA<br>1982<br>Best in show: Graphic Design<br>Honor Award: Publication<br>Honor Award: Business System | ▶ PRINTING HOUSE CRAFTSMEN'S CLUB<br>Chico, CA<br>1979 to 1982<br>Board of Directors, 1980<br>Graphic Coordinator, 1980<br>▶ DESIGNERS IN PROGRESS<br>California State University<br>Chico, CA<br>1979 to 1982<br>Steering Committee, 1980 |
| 1981 | ▶ ILLUSTRATOR CAMERA OPERATOR<br>Chico News & Review<br>Chico, CA<br>1981<br>Illustrated and designed editorial sections in weekly community news magazine. Operated horizontal copy camera. | ▶ | ▶ PRODUCTION ARTIST<br>Reber, Glenn, & Marz, Adv.<br>Reno, NV<br>1981<br>Designed, specified type, and produced camera ready artwork as full time intern. | | |
| 1980 | ▶ PRODUCTION ARTIST<br>DesignWare, Inc.<br>San Francisco, CA<br>1980<br>Worked as a member of production team for SRA Associates textbook/workbook "Computer Discovery" | | | | |
| 1979 | ▶ | ▶ CALIFORNIA STATE UNIVERSITY, CHICO<br>Chico, CA<br>1974 to 1979<br>B.A. Degree in Fine Arts, emphasis in drawing and watercolor. Graduated with Academic Distinction. | | | |

REFERENCES AVAILABLE

5879 pine view dr. paradise, ca. 95969

877-3949 for illustration and graphic design

**David Sherrod**

**experience:**
1/76-Present Freelance Illustration
1/78-6/78 Part-time Instructor, Art Center, College of Design, Pasadena, Ca.
7/74-10/75 Designer Illustrator, Dept. of Parks and Recreation, State of California

**education:**
Art Center College of Design, Pasadena, Ca., 1976-1977
California State University at Sacramento 1972-1974 BA–ART, minor–commercial art
Butte College, Durham, Ca., 1969-1971

**affiliations:**
1976-1978 ADLA, Art Directors Club of Los Angeles, Society of Illustrators of Los Angeles

**personal:**
Age 33, normal, healthy and unavailable for the draft

**client history:**
TRW magazine
Motor Trend magazine
Car Craft magazine
Hot Rod magazine
Skin Diver magazine
Let's Live magazine
Sundancer magazine
Bowmar Publishing – children's books
Diawa Inc.
Lowries Restaurant Corp.
Transcon Truck Lines
Global Marine International
Maxon Industrials
International Aluminum
May Co. Stores
Bullock's Stores

# HOT!

**Linda Clark Johnson**
553 South Campus Way
Davis, California 95616
916.756.2055

# EXPERIENCED

**Designer/Production Assistant**
Brian Collentine Graphic Design, San Francisco, CA, 1983 to 1985
As Mr. Collentine's assistant, my responsibilities on design projects included everything from ideation and concept development, through production. I worked directly with suppliers, typographers, printers and photographers, as well as clients. Accounts included Macys, I. Magnin, California Dental Service, The Sierra Club, Palo Alto Records and Passport Music Software.

**Designer**
Chico and San Francisco, CA, 1982 to 1983
As a freelance graphic designer and illustrator, I worked with the University (in Chico), many small businesses, a public relations firm, and other design firms.

**Lithographic Stripper**
Quadco Printing, Inc., Chico, CA, 1978 to 1983
Responsible for all complex film assembly, including four-color process, in quality commercial printing company. Also worked in art, camera, proofing, and platemaking departments. Created quality control system used in the plant. Supervised and trained other pre-press personnel.

**Illustrator/Camera Operator**
Chico News & Review, Chico, CA, 1981
Illustrated for editorial sections and performed all production camera work for weekly community news magazine.

**Production Artist**
Reber, Glenn & Marz Advertising, Reno, NV, 1981
Designed, specified type, and produced camera-ready artwork in agency.

# EDUCATED

**California State University, Chico**

**1979 to 1982** As a post graduate, I completed course work in graphic design, including publication design, corporate identity, typography, illustration, calligraphy, packaging, and creative problem solving. Designed show publicity posters for University Art Gallery.
Art directed staff of 6 for publication of annual student magazine, "Impulse."

**1974 to 1979** Received B.A. Degree in Fine Art with an emphasis in drawing and watercolor. Graduated with Academic Distinction.

# ACTIVE

**Organizations**

Art Directors and Artists Club, Sacramento, CA, 1979 to present
Attended Envision Conferences 6-10

Superior California Printing House Craftsmen, Chico, CA, 1979 to 1982
Board of Directors, 1980, Graphic Coordinator, 1980

Designers in Progress, California State University, Chico, 1979 to 1982
Steering Committee, 1980

**Awards**
Annual Design & Photography Show, California State University, Chico
1982 Best in Show: Graphic Design
Honor Award: Publication Design
Honor Award: Business System Design
1983 Honor Award: Calligraphy

# UNIQUE

Birthdate: December 12, 1955. I am currently happily married and in excellent health.
Some of my interests include calligraphy, knitting, letterwriting, bicycling, and museum-going.

**References available upon request.**

## Matthew Mizulo

## Special Teacher Report

To: Principal/Director
From: Ms. Thunderwood
Re: Matthew Mizulo
7 Dory Lane
Foster City, CA 94404
(415) 578-0309

I've compiled the following report because I feel that Matthew Mizulo is a real troublemaker. He has this strong work ethic and loyalty thing that defies description. There is also this little problem of an attitude. His attitude is, there is no place for second best. Even if he has to learn from his mistakes, he'll go out of his way to be number one. He definitely needs to be put in his place and a good place for him would be an entry-level position in your office.

The following report outlines four areas of concern.

## Drawing in Class

He's always drawing. Draw, draw, draw. I think it all began in the drafting class he took in high school. It quickly became all-consuming. He was drawing every spare moment he studied architecture at the College of San Mateo. I figured we had it licked when we confiscated his crayons and sent him to Paris, France to study European history and literature. Wrong again. That troublemaker Brunelleschi and his pals Michelangelo, Man-Ray, Lissitzky, Bayer and the rest of that motley crew dragged him further into the design world. He came back to the Academy of Art in San Francisco where I repeatedly caught him practicing design fundamentals. He went on to the California State University, Chico and drew himself right into a B.A. in Information and Communication Studies with an emphasis in graphic design.

2

## Taking Awards

On more than one occasion he's been caught taking awards. As a matter of fact, in 1991 at the California State University, Chico Visual Communication Show he took a gold medal in advertising design, a gold in typography design, a silver in package design and a bronze in publication design. More recently he swiped himself a spot on the Dean's List at CSUC with that little 3.66 GPA he has. His most audacious act was taking the grand prize in the Janet Turner Logo Design Contest in Chico. If it's possible, I'm willing to bet that someday he'll try and snag himself a few national awards using one of his crafty little designs.

3

## His Work

Every time I turn my back he's working. I've tried punishing him by keeping him late and giving him extra work, but he seems to power right through it...no problem. The little rascal seems to thrive on it.

Last year I caught him working at an exclusive wine and spirits shop called Foster's. While there, he got a stiff dose of how point of purchase displays and label designs affect peoples' buying decisions. When I caught up with him he was doing inventory tracking and control, wine tastings, processing customer inquiries, point of purchase displays, and sales.

Before that I witnessed him climbing his way up through Alpine Awards over a five-year period. He started with engraving and quickly found his way through silk-screen, photo-metal transfer, vertical camera operation and eventually ended up in their design department. He even had the gall to learn how to use the Macintosh and programs like Freehand, Illustrator, Pagemaker and Word. Next thing you know he'll learn Quark.

4

## Hanging Out

Rumor has it that Matt's been hanging out with some very influential people in these so called clubs. With his easily impressionable young mind, no telling what kind of positive influence they've wreaked upon him.

Recently he belonged to DIPS (Designers In Progress) whose clubhouse is in California State University, Chico. This club was extremely radical. On several occasions they invited guest speakers from larger clubs (sometimes referred to as firms) and held special lectures and workshops.

Prior to that Matt not only belonged to, but was president of a club called the American Institute of Architecture Students at the College of San Mateo.

It worries me that all this will lead to involvement in larger more powerful organizations like ADAC.

5

## Recommended Action

As the principal/director here, I feel you should have a long meaningful talk with this Matt Mizulo character. He's outside right now. Call for him at (415) 578-0309 and we'll march Mister Smarty Pants right in here and discuss this little business of design he's gotten himself into.

6

*The* **Cling** *variety of peach is known for its firm, not-so-sweet flesh that's treasured for its ability to hold up well under the heat and pressures of the canning process.*

**Laura Kling**

336 Broadway, Suite 24
Chico CA 95928
916.894.5125

**WORK EXPERIENCE**

1990
Graphic Design I
1986 to 1989
Graphic Designer
IMC Graphics, CSU Chico
Responsibilities include client consultation, design development, art direction of photographers, preparation of camera ready artwork for posters, brochures, logos, business systems and publications. Added responsibilities of Graphic Design I are shop management, art direction and training of student assistants.

1986 to the present
Kling Graphics
Reponsibilities include client consultation, illustration, design development, preparation of camera ready artwork, and print supervision of brochures, logos business systems, posters, publications, magazine covers, ads, and outdoor advertising.

1985 to 1989
Owner, Fruit Basket Upset
A business devoted to graphic rubber stamps. Responsibilities include management of business, accounting, manufacturing, supervision of contract labor, public relations, design and production of camera ready artwork for labels, ads, catalogs, and stamp images.

1978 to 1986
Production Manager
Zampa Design Studio
Designed, partcipated in and supervised the production of architectural etched glass panels and etched, painted sign systems. Also responsible for the hiring and training of employees, payroll, accounts payable and receivable.

Experienced with compugraphic headliner, Macintosh computer, vertical stat camera, and air brush

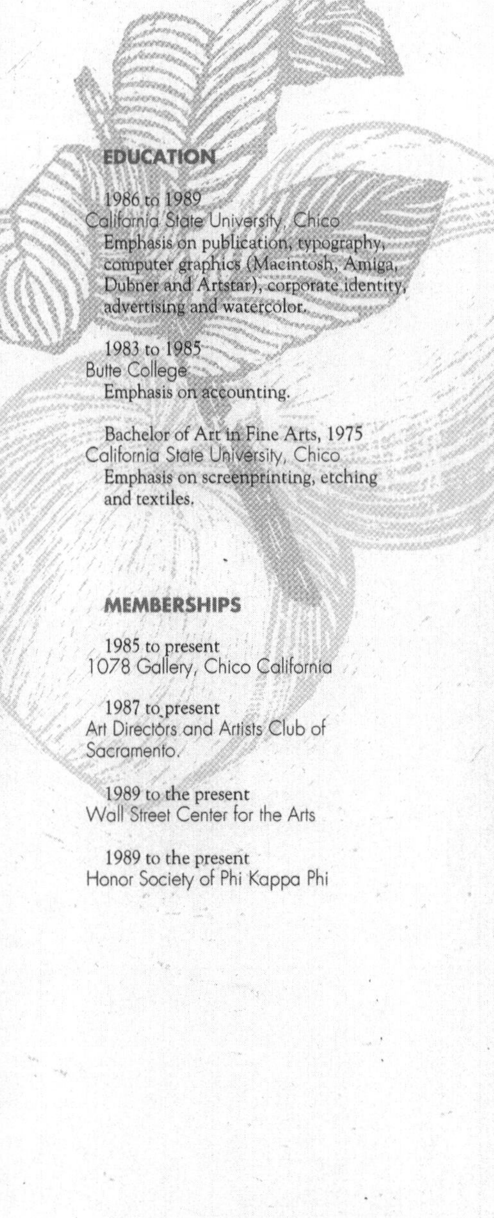

**EDUCATION**

1986 to 1989
California State University, Chico
Emphasis on publication, typography, computer graphics (Macintosh, Amiga, Dubner and Artstar), corporate identity, advertising and watercolor.

1983 to 1985
Butte College
Emphasis on accounting.

Bachelor of Art in Fine Arts, 1975
California State University, Chico
Emphasis on screenprinting, etching and textiles.

**MEMBERSHIPS**

1985 to present
1078 Gallery, Chico California

1987 to present
Art Directors and Artists Club of Sacramento.

1989 to the present
Wall Street Center for the Arts

1989 to the present
Honor Society of Phi Kappa Phi

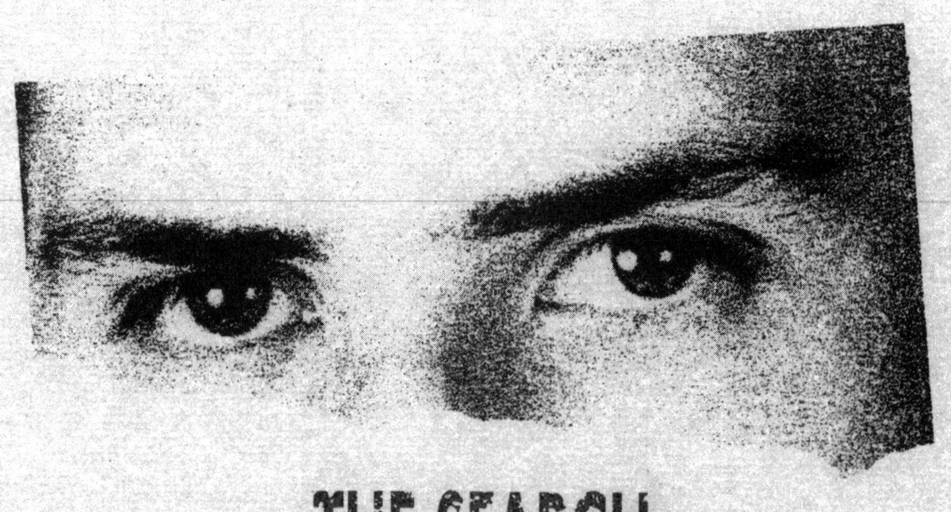

# THE SEARCH

STARRING

## CHRIS CARRIVEAU

1207 W. SACRAMENTO #8
CHICO, CALIFORNIA 95926
(916) 894-0854

## EDUCATION

CSU/CHICO, MONTANA STATE U. Department of Communication Design
BA Graphic Design • set design • graphic visualization • package design
photography • advertising design • typography • script writing • copywriting

## WORK EXPERIENCE

88 ADVERTISING ASSOCIATES
Chico, CA Intern
Paste up of brochures, newspaper ads
and operation of stat camera

89 INSTRUCTIONAL MEDIA CENTER
Chico State University, Intern involved in blue screen techniques
and model construction. Design production, and animation of
computer graphics using the Artstar, Abekas, and Dubner systems

87 STRAND UNION GRAPHICS
Montana State University
Client consultation, concept development
and production of camera ready art

## SPECIAL PROJECTS

Team production of a recreational video in stress relief • Co-Owner "TOO HUGE" fashions, beachwear • Produced a multi-image show "The Fairmont, San Francisco"

Assisted with production of projects including video, film, slide/tape, graphics and titles for student films, and set design

## HONORS AND AFFILIATIONS

Society of Motion Picture & Television Engineers (SMPTE) • Designers in Progress (DIPS)

C.S.U. CHICO STUDENT DESIGN SHOW FIRST PLACE 1989

R | RESUME | REFERENCES UPON REQUEST ®

COMING SOON
TO YOUR AREA

**1** .75 year of full time, professional design work

**EMPLOYMENT**

Associate Art Director
Elliott/Dickens - San Jose, CA (1 year)
Magazine Ads, Packaging, Logos, Publications, Direct Response, Photo Shoots, Multimedia Presentations.
Clients: Hewlett-Packard, Insignia Solutions, Macromedia, Seiko, Technique Magazine.

Graphics Lab Assistant
Presentation Graphics Lab - IMC (2 years) Service Bureau, CSU Chico, CA
Design Consulting, Canon Color Printing/Copying/Scanning, Vynl Cutting, Video Editing, Multimedia Presentations.

Creative Intern
MMS Design/Jack Nadel Inc. - Oakland, CA (Summer 1993)
Incentive Marketing Programs, Direct Response, Logos, Brochures.
Clients: PowerBar, SCO

Production Artist
Team Design - Walnut Creek, CA (Summer 1992)
Publications, Newspaper Ads, Speed training in Quark XPress.
Clients: Sears, Yardbirds, Meeks, Serta

**AWARDS/ACTIVITIES**

First place in logo design contest for Chico Association of Realtors, Inc. with 26 participants:
Wrote contract and design brief, Designed business system and other applications, Presented logo system to client, Received award and was hired for further design.

Member of Designers in Progress:
Participated in specialty design seminars, lectures by renowned members of the field and weekly meetings and activities.

Member of Marketing Association:
Attended marketing seminars and weekly meetings.

Racer on the Chico State Alpine Ski Team:
Designed T-shirts and other applications.

Member of GDI (co-ed social and community service group):
Chairperson of Media Committee, During term, designed all advertisements and T-shirts.

**EDUCATION**

California State University, Chico; Bachelor of Arts degree in Communications with an option in Graphic Design, May 1994.
Design GPA 3.5.

Studies included Package, Publication, and Corporate Design systems, Advertising, Copywriting, Typography (1 & 2), Letterforms, Graphic Design History, Photography, Pre-Press, Scriptwriting, Color Theory, Research and Criticism.

Passed Portfolio Review (acceptance to major) as one of 18 out of 72 people who applied, Fall 1990.

**MACINTOSH SKILLS**

Fast and efficient computer aided design.

Experience using:

| | |
|---|---|
| Quark XPress 3.31 | Illustrator 5.5 |
| Photoshop 3.0 | Macromedia Freehand 5.0 |
| Pagemaker 3.0 | Macromedia Authorware |
| Streamline 3.0 | Macromedia Fontographer |

Aimee Lynne Dale, 408.298.2650, 260 N.3rd Street, Suite F, San Jose, CA 95112

## "LET'S DO LUNCH"

Jess Giambroni / Graphic Design
4111 Rhoda Ave / Oakland, CA. 94602
415 531 3310 / 916 527 5659

## "APPETIZERS"

1990

California State University, Chico: Visual communications - Courses studied: Corporate identity, Advertising design, Publication design, Typography, Illustration, Copywriting, Photography

1986

Butte College, Chico: AA Degree Liberal Arts

## "ENTREES"

1990 - 1991

Landor Associates, San Francisco: Junior Freelance Designer - Assited with the design, development and production of corporate identity programs.

1990

Landor Associates, San Francisco: Design Intern - Created and developed corporate identity concepts, designs and systems for domestic and international companies. Experienced acquired: Design team interaction, strengthened knowlege of corporate identity, production and computer skills.

1989 - 1990

Giambroni Design, Red Bluff: Freelance Designer - Provided design services for local and regional companies. Services provided: Corporate identity, packaging and advertising.

1989

Chico News & Review Newspaper, Chico: Illustration Intern - Created and executed illustrations for editorial columns, commentaries and advertisements. Experienced acquired: Increased creative ability and awareness, developed illustration techniques and enhanced drawing skills.

## "DESSERTS"

1990

California State University, Chico: Annual Student Show - Honor: T-shirt design, Honor: Publication design, Honor: Typography, Honor: Advertising design

1989

California State University, Chico: Annual Student Show - Best of show: Advertising illustration, Honor: Color illustration, Honor: Typography

1989 - 1990

California State University, Chico: "Designers In Progress" student design group - President and Executive Director

## "SIDE ORDERS"

Available upon request

Graphic Design
**Visual Communications**
Photography


203 446 6690

**Lance Westin**
22 East Holly Street
New Haven CT 06522


9/77 . 5/79
**Yale University, New Haven CT**
typography, drawing oriented design, color, photography, book design, letterform design, bookbinding, magazine/publication design
**MFA 1979**
Alvin Eisenman, Paul Rand, Norman Ives, Armin Hofmann, Herbert Matter, Bradbury Thompson, Alan Fletcher, Andre Gurtler, Inge Druckrey, Christopher Pullman
**Graphic Design**
academic courses in geology, natural resources, archaeology

10/76 . 9/77
**University of Massachusetts, Boston MA**
university released publications, audiovisual/video graphics, environmental graphics
**Visual Information Designer**

5/76 . 9/76
**Benjamin Thompson+Associates, Cambridge MA**
environmental graphics
**Graphic Designer**

9/72 . 5/76
**Yale University, New Haven CT**
drawing, design, printmaking, photography, typography, color
**BA 1976**
academic courses in mathematics, psychology, anthropology, sociology, classical civilization
**Art**

2/55
**born, Philadelphia PA**

references available upon request

## MATHEW JACOBS

523 West Fourth Ave
Chico, CA 95926
(916) 892-9027

## EDUCATION

**1996 MA** Instructional Technology & Design
**1990 BA** Graphic Design
California State University, Chico

**Fluent in Mac and PC Environments**
Quark XPress, Illustrator, Photoshop, PageMaker
PageMill, Powerpoint, Persuasion, Word, Works, more.

## AWARDS / SHOWS

**First Place** National Collegiate Press
National University Publication Web Page 1996
**First Place** Print Magazine, Symbol System 1993
**First Place** Chico Art Show, Architectural Photo 1990
**First Place** CSUC Annual Poster Competition 1989
**Gallery Exhibition** CSUC Fine Art Gallery
Illustration & Photography 1988

## FREELANCE

**Design and Production for a variety of clients including:**
Landor Associates (SF), San Francisco Giants, California Dept. of Forestry, Swensen's, Clement Mok (SF), Bayshore Magazine, VideoMaker Magazine, California Board of Registered Nursing

**Graphic Design skills**
packaging, publications, identity, concept to press, project management, art direction, print management, team player, deadline maker, production and consulting

**Instructional Development skills**
instructional design management, training, proposals, needs/goal assessment and analysis, learning objectives, strategy and tests, implementation, motivation, evaluation

bilingual in American Sign Language, six trips through Europe, enjoy skiing, mt. biking, hiking, music

*references available upon request*

## EXPERIENCE

**1996** **Art Director/Graphic Design** Congressional Campaign
*Identity, Publications, Environmental design*

**1995-96** **Graphic Design** The Orion, Chico, CA
*Advertising and Supplement design, Web Page design*

**1993-95** **Art Director/Graphic Design**
International Microcomputer Software Inc. (IMSI), Marin, CA
*Packaging, Publications, Identity, CD-ROMs, Advertisements, Trade Show Systems, Project Management, Freelance Management, Photo Direction*

**1992-93** **Graphic Design** Vicom / FCB, San Francisco, CA
*Advertising design and production*

**1991-92** **Graphic Design** IMC Graphics, Chico, CA
*Publication and Slide Show design and production*

**1989-90** **Senior Designer** Union Graphics, Chico, CA
*Publications, Identity, Posters, Advertisements, Design and Intern Management*

**1986-88** **AutoCAD Technician**
Erin Engineering, Walnut Creek, CA
*Plumbing and Electrical Diagrams for power plants*

**Tom Bross** **916.852.1263** **10601 Coliseum Way** **Rancho Cordova, CA 95670**

*Infinite potential to grow...*

Hello. I'm Tom Bross, Director of Advertising for Merksamer Jewelers, a retail chain with 48 stores nationwide. **Not your everyday ad nut,** my goal is to work alongside other accomplished professionals, learn new aspects of the trade and contribute to the creation of successful visual communications.

My **dedication, experience and talents** are offered in exchange for this professional growth.

*pushing creative boundaries...*

My interest in the business may have sprouted from an appearance in a Clorox commercial at age 8. I was paid to wear a mustard stain and a grin. This positive experience left me more **sensitive and critical of advertising** in general. (Well, that's what I told my parents when I was watching too much television... ) While I was growing up, my family traveled quite a bit. We even had a small bus instead of a station wagon. The kids at school used to call us the *Partridge Family*; I told them they watched way too much TV. Besides, come summer, everyone wanted to tag along on our trips.

**At CSU, Chico, I supported myself** by managing apartment complexes and throwing Rico's Pizzas. I made good dough. As an **intern at Advertising Associates**, a small full-service agency, I helped with print production, storyboarding, creating props, video production... you name it. I also began working as a **freelance designer** while still in school. **I graduated with honors in 1986**, with a **BA in Communications/Graphic Design.**

In my first "real" job at Chico's Quadco Printing, I was **Designer, Production Artist, Camera Operator and Pre-press Assistant** all in one shell. I worked directly with clients to design a variety of printed pieces from start to finish. I learned the intricacies of printing that allowed me to take my solutions to press successfully. I was active in the **Chico Ad Club** and maintained my freelance clientele.

After a couple of years I was ready for the meatier challenges of a larger market. This led to my position as **Art Director for Merksamer Jewelers** in Sacramento. Thus began my career in retail advertising—the frontline trenches of the trade.

As Art Director, **I developed creative concepts and oversaw production,** while supervising a staff of five. I've met many impossible deadlines, while maintaining high morale among my employees and clients. Sharpening my technical skills, I learned to style and art-direct critical photography. I also learned how to effectively market our product. **In 1990, I was promoted to Creative Director.**

Now I'm responsible for all aspects of marketing Merksamer Jewelers to the public. I develop **print and radio ads, point-of-purchase materials, catalogs** and other print collateral. I manage **media** buys and **mailing lists.** I coordinate "lease-required" store **promotions.** I develop and manage my department's **budget, schedule and all subcontracts.** I also support other departments on various in-house projects, and—oh yes—keep up with the paperwork.

I've implemented money-saving efficiencies for the company. **I've enhanced the image of Merksamer Jewelers** with the quality of our communications.

*a major professional breakthrough...*

When you get a call from a nut like this, schedule a break and crack open my portfolio. I'll even bring a copy of the Clorox ad if you wish! You might say that ad planted the advertising seed. Now I'm ripe for transplant—ready to apply my **talents and energy** to a crop of **new challenges.**

*poised for new challenges...*

**CHRISTINA VAQUERA DELL'AGOSTINO**

GRAPHIC DESIGNER

301 18TH AVENUE Nº5
SAN FRANCISCO ▲ CALIFORNIA
94121

415 ▲ 752 ▲ 9476


## EXPERIENCE

**Program Designer**
March 1992-October 1993
*Sacramento News & Review*
Sacramento, California

Created ads programs, special supplements and promotional pieces for award-winning weekly alternative newspaper.

**Freelance Designer**
January-February 1992
*Tackett-Barbaria Design*
Sacramento, California

Assisted in design & production of projects for graphic design studio.

**Bilingual Teacher's Assistant**
Summers 1989 & 1990
*California Mini-Corps*
Sacramento, California

Supervised & tutored migrant children in ESL, math and art.

**Ad Design Assistant**
March-December 1988
*Action Advertising Agency*
Chico, California

Designed & produced print advertising.

**Production Person**
June 1986-March 1988
*Glenn-Colusa Newspapers*
Willows, California

Layout & typesetting for two bi-weekly publications.

## INTERNSHIPS

**Design Intern**
July-December 1991
*Tackett-Barbaria Design*
Sacramento, California

Production & design of studio projects.

**Design Intern**
August-December 1989
*College of the Humanities*
California State University, Chico, California

Designed & produced posters for university events.

**Design Intern**
Summer 1985
*Chico News & Review*
Chico, California

Ad design & paste-up of a weekly publication.

## EDUCATION

**California State University, Chico, California**
**December 1991**

**BA Visual Communications Graphic Design Emphasis.**
Typography, Graphic Viz, Reprographics, Package Design, Advanced Typography, Advertising Design, Advertising Copywriting, Corporate Design and Publication Design.

## COMPUTER EXPERIENCE

Aldus Freehand 3.1
Aldus Pagemaker 4.2
Adobe Illustrator 3.0
Adobe Photoshop 2.5
Microsoft Word 2.0
QuarkXPress 3.11

## SPECIAL COURSES

**University of California, Davis, California**
Spring 1992
*Business Skills for Graphic Design Professionals*
Instructor:
Paul Page of
Page Design,
Sacramento, California

**California State University, Chico, California**
Spring 1991
*Design Workshop*
Instructor:
Michael Kennedy of
Michael Kennedy Design,
Sacramento, California

## LANGUAGES

**Spanish and English**
(spoken & written)

## MEMBERSHIPS

**Art Directors & Artist's Club**
1992-1993
Sacramento, California

**Designers In Progress**
1988-1991
California State University, Chico, California

**Latinos In Technical Careers**
1986-1987
California State University, Chico, California

## AWARDS

**Recipient of Graphic Design Scholarship**
1991
California State University, Chico, California

**Recipient of Hispanic Association for the Community & Education Scholarship**
1986
Chico, California

## REFERENCES

Available upon request

# Jacob Early

530 8933407

*5 Firefly Court - Chico, California 95926*

jearly@telis.org


*p r o f e s s i o n a l*

**December 1995 - May 1997**
Jacob Early Design
Owner

**January 1996 - Present**
Northern California Trails Magazine
Art Director & Co-Founder
Eric Moore, Publisher 530. 898-1032

**February 1993 - January 1996**
Media Screenprint
Designer
Bob Malowney, Owner 530. 893-0545

*e d u c a t i o n*

**1994**
**Bachelor of Arts, Graphic Design, CSU, Chico**

1992
La Facultàd de Bellas Artes, Sevilla, España
Fine Arts College, University of Seville, Spain

*d i g i t a l*

| **Macintosh** | OS 8 |
|---|---|
| | Freehand<br>Photoshop<br>Quark<br>Streamline<br>Fontographer<br>Microsoft Word |
| | America Online<br>Netscape Navigator |

*r e f e r e n c e s*

Steve Gilmore
Architect
Lassen Design Studio
530. 474-3366

Gregg Berryman
Professor
CSU, Chico
530. 898-6872

Dan Dewayne
Maple Creek Presents
530. 891-4081

Product Identity
RM Enterprises
Tokyo, Japan

Identity
Retail Importer
Chico, CA

Logo
Lan Mark Computers
RM Enterprises
Tokyo, Japan

Mark
Bird In Hand
Chico, CA

Logo & Identity System
Seismic Industries
Chico, CA

Logo & Masthead
Trails Magazine
Chico, CA

**Alan Rellaford**

Resume

1850 Humboldt Road #44
Chico, California
95928
530/892.8672

**E x p e r i e n c e**

**5/99 - Present**
**Design Director**
**Tourism and Communication Design Partnership**
**CSU, Chico University Foundation**

In conjunction with teaching responsibilities, I serve as design director for a variety of projects for government agencies which contract with the University Foundation. Through an innovative partnership with Recreation department faculty, I supervise student designers in creating solutions to tourism related problems. As a result, clients receive the benefits of professional-level design for a fraction of the cost, and students obtain valuable professional experience.
**Clients: Bureau of Land Management, Caltrans, Sacramento Area Parks and Recreation, USDA Forest Service**

**1/97 - Present**
**Lecturer, Graphic Design**
**California State University, Chico**
**Chico, California**

As an instructor in the Graphic Design Program, I am responsible for developing class lectures, assignments and curriculum, and coordinating guest speakers and field trips. Studio class curriculum is comprised of a variety of hands-on projects for theoretical and actual clients. I regularly evaluate and advise students on their progress and on career options following graduation. In addition, I serve as faculty adviser to Designers In Progress, the student design organization.
**Classes taught: Corporate Identity Systems, Publication Design, Advanced Typography, Computer Graphics for the Macintosh, Creative Problem Solving.**

**9/89 - 10/96**
**Senior Design Director**
**Sargent & Berman**
**Santa Monica, California**

As Senior Design Director, I managed a variety of projects including packaging, corporate identity systems, advertising, collateral systems and naming. In addition, I served as a project director - developing strong working relationships with clients, writing proposals, estimating and billing, tracking projects, and preparing and giving presentations. In these capacities, I worked in close partnership with the principals developing new business opportunities, leading the design and production staff, managing computer systems and supervising printers and photographers.
**Clients: Sunkist, The Franklin Mint, Princess Cruises, The Upper Deck Company, Teleflora, Glendale Adventist Medical Center, Florida Hospital, World Cup Soccer 1994, Samtron Monitors, MITI, Eldon/Rubbermaid, Pep Products.**

**1/90 - 6/90**
**Instructor**
**Art Center College of Design**
**Pasadena, California**

I taught a weekly, full-day basic design and advertising class for second and third term students as part of Art Center's foundation program. Under the direction of the Associate Dean, I prepared lectures and assignments, evaluated and critiqued student work, coordinated guest speakers and field trips, and met with the students on campus during the week to evaluate their progress.

**3/87 - 9/89**
**Project Director/Senior Designer**
**Bright and Associates**
**Santa Monica, California**

As Project Director, I co-managed a national corporate identity program for Ryder Truck Rental, incorporating system nomenclature, vehicle identity, facility signing, retail interiors, collateral and packaging. I supervised a staff of 10 designers and production artists while maintaining an extensive travel schedule to conduct presentations and meetings with senior management and to supervise implementation throughout the U.S. with a variety of vendors at numerous client sites. In addition, I served as senior designer on an identity program for National Car Rental, providing creative input to team management and preparing and presenting to all levels of client management.
**Clients: Ryder Truck Rental, National Car Rental, Sail America Foundation, Northrop**

**10/83 -11/86**
**Designer**
**Landor Associates**
**San Francisco, California**

I designed corporate identities, identity systems, design and production management of several graphic standards manuals. Created brand/product names, developed project management and presentation skills, became skilled operator of Dicomed Imaginator Computer System (before the Mac!) served as president of Landor Employee Committee, coordinated company activities and served as primary contact with management and human resources department.
**Clients: Pacific Telesis Group/Pacific Bell, American Medical International, OTC Australia, italiatour!, BR Toys, Van Leer, Oral B, Nobel Industries, GE, Sitmar Cruises**

**1993 . . . . .**

*Group Four Design*
*Design Manager – responsible for the creative development of brand identity programs, retail packaging, collateral print, and providing graphic support to the product design department*

**1991 . 1993**

*gS Design*
*• Principal – developing corporate identity and consumer packaging programs for clients within the U.S. and Canadian markets*
*• Freelance consultant to local design firms requiring managerial and/or creative assistance with corporate identity and package design programs*

**1983 . 1991**

*Landor Associates*
*Design Director – responsible for developing project proposals, managing the design and implementation of client programs, tracking project budgets, maintaining long-term relationships with clients and implementation suppliers, and assisting in new business development*

**1978 . 1983**

*S&O Consultants*
*Project Director – responsible for general project management including client contact, design development, evaluation and presentation of creative work, budget control, and program implementation*

**1973 . 1978**

*Container Corporation of America*
*Designer • Photographer – responsible for conceptual design development, creating reproduction art, maintaining photo studio, and producing slide presentations*

## PROFESSIONAL ORGANIZATIONS

*AIGA*

## EDUCATION

*California State University, Chico, 1973, Bachelor of Science in Graphic Communication with a minor in Marketing*

## RETAIL PACKAGING

*Alex Foods*
*AlliedSignal Corporation*
*Anheuser Busch*
*Blitz Wienhard Beer*
*Blue Diamond Almonds*
*Caterpillar Inc.*
*Chevron Chemical Company*
*Del Monte Corporation*
*Kendall-Futuro Company*
*Konica Corporation USA*
*Liberty House*
*Mrs. Fields Cookies*
*Omark Industries*
*PacTel Products*
*Pisano French Bread*
*Purex Corporation*
*Russell Athletic Corporation*
*Valent USA*

## CORPORATE & BRAND IDENTITY

*ACCO World Corporation*
*Anheuser Busch*
*America's Cup - USA*
*Bank of America - Versatel*
*Caterpillar Inc.*
*Librex Computers (Nippon Steel)*
*Kloster Cruise Limited*
*Mrs. Fields Cookies*
*Norwegian Cruise Line*
*Pacific Telesis/Pacific Bell*
*Raytel Medical Corporation*
*Transamerica Corporation*
*20th Century Fox*
*Valent USA (Chevron/Sumitomo)*
*The Concord Pavillion*
*Tong Yang (Korea)*
*Chuo Trust Bank (Japan)*
*Orix Corportation (Japan)*
*OTC Telecommunications(Australia)*
*Sistemi Urbani (Italy)*

## DESIGNER . CREATIVE MANAGER

*Twenty-one years experience developing and managing all aspects of corporate identity and packaging programs for clients across a broad range of business categories in domestic and overseas markets*

. . . . . . . . . . . . .

**GREG SILVERIA**
*21 Chatsworth Rd.*
*Granby, CT 06035*
*203.653.7330*

*Karen Ann*
*328 Rutledge Street*
*San Francisco,*
*California 94110*
*415.285.3875*

**EXPERIENCE**

**KAREN ANN DESIGN**

*July 1995 to the present*

Because of my interest in pursuing new career goals in education, I am working part-time in my graphic design business. I am currectly producing newsletters for two clients, Adobe Systems and Autodesk.

**FULCRUM DESIGN**

*July 1992 to July 1995*

My partner and I began this graphic design business which specialized in print and multimedia projects. These projects included packaging, point-of-purchase materials, brochures, posters, newsletters, identity systems, and sales and training demonstrations. Clients included Apple Computer, CNN, Pacific Bell, Intel Corporation, Adobe Systems, Liberty Mutual, Autodesk and Long's Drugs.

**ADOBE SYSTEMS INCORPORATED**

*July 1988 to July 1992*

Adobe develops software for use by graphic designers. The in-house marketing group produces promotional materials for these products. Beginning as a designer, I produced packaging and brochures. Later, as an art director, I was in charge of packaging and sales promotion, and thus supervised projects and managed a staff of five. My responsibilities also included public speaking, giving demonstrations and teaching.

**AKAGI DESIGN**

*July 1987 to July 1988*

As senior designer for this graphic design studio, I worked in collaboration with the principal from initiation to completion of each project. Beside concept, design and production, I was also involved in business aspects, especially estimating and budget management. I was responsible for print production, which included writing print specifications, acquiring bids, reviewing proofs and press checking. Clients included PacTel InfoSystems, U.S. Leasing Corporation and various architectural firms.

**FREELANCE**

*September 1984 to July 1987*

My freelance business consisted of working for graphic design studios and marketing firms. I was involved in all areas of design from initial concept to mechanicals. Projects included logo development, corporate systems, promotional brochures and posters. Clients included Pentagram, The Office of Michael Manwaring and Landor Associates.

**PICKETT COMMUNICATIONS**

*November 1983 to June 1984*

This marketing firm specializes in collateral materials, packaging and sales promotion. As staff designer I was responsible for concept development, design, art direction and project management. Clients included Levi Strauss, DHL Corporation and Apple Computers.

**UNIGRAPHICS**

*August 1981 to September 1983*

This design firm produced annual reports and corporate graphics. As part of a team, I assisted with concept and design, and controlled the production management. My responsibilities included project research, preparation of comprehensives, type specification, mechanicals, color proofing and press checking. Duties also included client contact, writing cost estimates and schedules, and the hiring and management of freelance personnel.

**TEACHING**

California College of Arts and Crafts 1991-92, Kent State University Summer Seminar 1992, AIGA Conference 1989 and 1991, Adobe Invitationals 1990, Aspen Design Conference 1990

**EDUCATION**

San Francisco State University, Masters of Arts in Art Education, ongoing
California College of Arts and Crafts, Program for Graphic Design, 1986
San Francisco State University, B.A. Magna Cum Laude, Special Major in Art and Industry, 1978

**AWARDS AND PUBLICATIONS**

Print 1993: *Computer Art and Design Annual 2,* AIGA 1991: *Graphic Design USA 12, International Typography Almanac 1991,* Print 1991: *Regional Design Annual* and *Computer Art and Design Annual 1,* Type Directors Club 1991: *Typography 12,* San Francisco Art Director's Club 1988, *American Corporate Identity 5* and *6,* Communication Arts 1986: *CA Design Annual*

Member of AIGA
References and portfolio available on request.

# Bob Dahlquist

*Graphic Designer*
*& Typographer*

3728 McKinley Blvd.
Sacramento, California
95816.3418

Telephone + Fax:
916.736.9550

E-mail:
bobshaus@aol.com

**Experience**

1989 to present — PRINCIPAL, *Bob's Haus, Sacramento*
The studio's focus is typographic design solutions and business identity. Clients include *Before & After Magazine*, Berkeley Mills Furniture Company, Chronicle Books, Nacht & Lewis Architects, and the Sacramento Ballet.

1986 to 1989 — GRAPHIC DESIGNER, *Tackett-Barbaria Design, Sacramento*
Responsibilities included design and production of corporate identities, packaging, posters, brochures, annual reports, advertising and exhibits; client consultation and art direction of photographers and freelancers. Clients included Intel Corporation, Hewlett-Packard, the State of California, and the Sacramento Zoo.

1984 to 1986 — ART DIRECTOR, *Teleguide, Sacramento*
Overseeing a staff of four designers, my responsibilities included the implementation and maintenance of graphic standards, "page" design, company signage, vehicle identity and terminal kiosk graphics, as well as the company's printed materials.

*A precursor to our present use of the Internet, Teleguide was an experimental videotex operation of McClatchy Newspapers, using signals sent through phone lines to remote interactive color terminals.*

1983 to 1984 — GRAPHIC DESIGNER, *Pat Davis Design, Sacramento*

**Education**

1983 — BACHELOR *of* ARTS DEGREE, *Visual Communications*, CSU, CHICO

**Activities**

1996 — GUEST JUDGE & LECTURER, *Annual Student Show*, CSU, CHICO

FEATURE ARTICLE SUBJECT, *Step-by-Step Graphics, Vol. 12, #3*

1995 — CONFERENCE SPEAKER, *Envision 21 Design Conference*, Sacramento

ATTENDEE, *ATypI International Typography Conference*, Barcelona

1994 — LECTURER, *On Typography*, sponsored by ADAC, Sacramento

1993 — LECTURER, *Dangerous Banana* student conference, CSU, SACRAMENTO

1992 to 1995 — GUEST LECTURER, *CSU, Sacramento* (Deborah Zemke); *American River College* (Betty Nelson); *Sacramento City College* (Kathy Noonan)

References are available on request.

2422 Oregon Street Berkeley, California 94705 415-548-2974

**Richard Garnas**

*Objective:*
*Senior Designer*
*Project Manager*

***Professional Experience***

*1977–Present*
*Barile/Garnas Design*
*Oakland, California*
*Principal*

*Project Management:*

*Consulting with client to establish project focus and performance expectations; skilled at asking pertinent questions, listening and developing solid strategies.*

*Conducting research on client structure and product, markets and competition; capable of assessing the facts and grasping the overview.*

*Devising schedule and budget parameters; experienced at managing long-term projects with six figure budgets.*

*Managing design and production work-flow, including regular progress reports; consistent at meeting deadlines and achieving quality results.*

*Design Approach:*

*Applying the principle of form following function, incorporating marketing goals and budget limitations.*

*Employing problem-solving skills that go beyond given criteria for each project.*

*Projects:*

*Corporate identity and standards manuals*

*Internal communications*

*Signage and interior graphics*

*Computer software manuals*

*Packaging*

*Collateral including annual reports, capabilities brochures, marketing literature, data sheets, direct mail and posters*

*Partial Client List:*

*Apple Computer, AT&T, Celestial Software Inc., Herman Miller Inc., IBM, Impell Corporation, Landor Associates, Light Language Photography, Security Pacific Leasing Corporation*

*1972–1977*
*Communications Design Inc.*
*Sacramento, California*

*Project Manager:*

*Performed key role in developing team concept in studio organization. Staff grew from four to twenty people and project budgets increased twentyfold during tenure.*

*Produced work-flow management systems.*

*Assumed full project responsibility from client introduction to completed product. Personally accountable for project profitability.*

*Additional responsibilities included client consultation, project budgeting, research, design and supervision of all phases of production.*

*Firm was eventually acquired by Citicorp, New York.*

*Affiliations:*

*One of the founders of "Envision," an annual design symposium in Sacramento, California, that presents to students and professionals a microcosm of current developments in art and design. Now celebrating its eleventh year, it has become one of the most successful conferences of its kind. The proceeds provide funding for professional workshops and student scholarships.*

***Education***

*1984*
*Peter Rogen & Associates*
*New York, New York*
*Seminar*
*Sales Presentation Techniques*

*BFA, 1972*
*Kansas City Art Institute*
*Kansas City, Missouri*
*Major: Graphic Design*
*Honors: Deans List*

*BA, 1967*
*University of Iowa*
*Iowa City, Iowa*
*Major: Liberal Arts/Fine Arts*

***Shows***

*1985*
*Kansas City Art Institute*
*100 Year Retrospective*
*The Nelson-Atkins Museum of Art*
*Kansas City, Missouri*

*1971*
*Photography Exhibit*
*Rourke Gallery*
*Moorehead, Minnesota*

***Published Work***

*Art Direction Magazine*

*Art Directors Club of Los Angeles*

*Communications Arts Annual*

*Graphis Poster Annual*

*Mead Library of Ideas Exhibition*

*Photographis*

*Print Magazine*

*San Francisco Society of Communicating Arts*

*The American Institute of Graphic Arts*

*New York Art Directors Club*

*New York Type Directors Club*

*The Western Art Directors Club*

***References***

*Available upon request.*

*Sandra McHenry*

| | *Experience* | *Education* | *Awards* |
|---|---|---|---|
| 81 | **Ross Design/ Opus Group** Design and production of corporate identity programs, annual reports, collateral materials, catalogs, books, magazines and advertising. Responsibilities included client contact, press checks, photo art direction, maintenance of production schedules, supervision of other employees. | | |
| 80 | | | |
| 79 | | | |
| 78 | **Lawrence Bender and Associates** Design and production of annual reports, corporate brochures, corporate magazines and collateral material. | **Kent Summer in Switzerland** Color, drawing and representation, typography, and form | **Communication Arts Society of Los Angeles Certificate of Merit** |
| 77 | **California State University, Chico Instructional Media Center** Directed application of University's identity to publications, signage, business forms. Helped develop sub-systems for institutes, grants. Planned type systems for catalogues, new publications, posters. Scripted multi-media program for use in graphic design program. | | **UCDA Excellence Award**<br>**California State University Chancellor's Grant Conference for design professionals in the university and college system. Emphasis was placed on the improvement and quality of design as applied to a university's visual communications.** |
| 76 | | | |
| 75 | | **California State University, Chico Graduate Program** Film and TV, Drawing Illustration, Printmaking, Psychology | **UCDA Excellence Award*** UCDA Gold Award**<br>**UCDA Silver Award UCDA Merit Award** |
| 74 | **Unique Printing, Chico** Prepared camera ready art, operated IBM typesetting machine, plate-making machine. | **California State University, Chico Graphic Design Visual Communications June 1974 Bachelor of Arts** Packaging, corporate identity, typography, advertising, information systems, photomechanical reproduction, black and white and color photography | |
| 73 | **Block Printing, Chico** Prepared camera ready art, typesetting for books, posters, catalogs, brochures. | | |
| 72 | | | |
| 71 | | | |
| 70 | | **Montana State University Industrial Design—Firenze Summer Program** Art History, Industrial Design | |
| 1969 | | **Montana State University** Industrial design, interior design, architecture, graphic design, ceramics, drawing, painting | |

# Resume Bibliography


Designing Creative Resumes
Gregg Berryman
Menlo Park, CA
Crisp Publications

Resumes for
Advertising Careers
VGM Career Horizons
Lincolnwood, IL
NTC Publishing Group

The Perfect Resume
Tom Jackson
New York, NY
Anchor Press/Doubleday

The Damn Good
Resume Guide
Yana Parker
Berkeley, CA
Ten Speed Press


# Portfolio Bibliography


Designing Creative Portfolios
Gregg Berryman
Menlo Park, CA
Crisp Publications

How to Put Your Book
Together and Get a Job in
Advertising
Maxine Paetro
New York, NY
Copy Workshop

The Advertising Portfolio
Ann Marie Barry
New York, NY
McGraw Hill

The Perfect Portfolio
Henrietta Brackman
New York, NY
Watson-Guptill

Out of Print/Try library
or used bookstore:

The Graphic Design Portfolio
Paula Scher
New York, NY
Watson-Guptill

The Ultimate Portfolio
Martha Metzdorf
Cincinnati, OH
North Light Books


# Career Bibliography


Becoming A Graphic Designer
Heller & Fernandes
New York, NY
John Wiley & Sons

Careers By Design
Roz Goldfarb
New York, NY
Allworth Press

Graphic Design:
A Career Guide &
Education Directory
AIGA
New York, NY
Watson-Guptill

Out of Print/Try library or
used bookstore:

Breaking Into Advertising
Ken Musto
New York, NY
Van Nostrand Reinhold

Designing Business
Clement Mok
San Jose, CA
Adobe Press

Design Career
Heller & Talarico
New York, NY
Van Nostrand Reinhold

Graphic Design Career Guide
James Craig
New York, NY
Watson-Guptill

The School of Visual Arts
Guide to Careers
Dee Ito
New York, NY
McGraw Hill


# Placement Agencies

Aquent Online
www.aquent.com

Communications Arts
www.creativehotlist.com
www.designinteract.com

The Creative Group
www.creativegroup.com

Creative Resource
www.thecreativeresource.com

Roz Goldfarb Associates
www.rga-joblink.com

Graphxstaff
www.graphxstaff.com

Janou Parker, Inc.
www.janouparker.com

Monster.com
www.monster.com

Paladin Staffing
www.paladinstaff.com

RitaSue Siegel Resources
www.ritasuesiegelresources.com

Stone & Co.
www.stoneandco.com

Wert and Compamy
www.wertco.com